TRAIL & ERROR

A Rookie Outdoor Woman's Path to Rediscovering Adventure and Confidence After 50

HEIDI BONNER

ISBN **979-8-9938276-1-2** (pbk)
ISBN **979-8-9938276-2-9** (hcv)
ISBN **979-8-9938276-0-5** (ebook)

Library of Congress Control Number: **2025925717**

This book cracked me open in the best way. Heidi Bonner writes about rebuilding a life after loss with honesty and humor that make it feel less like a memoir and more like a real conversation. There's no performance here. Just someone telling the truth about what it takes to begin again.
Aaron Poynton | Bestselling Author, *Think Like A Black Sheep*

Trail & Error is a life survival guide particularly for Generation X women and certainly for midlife women navigating divorce. Heidi Bonner provides you with the map and the tools in a refreshingly realistic way. I especially liked the Trail Truths, Field Notes, Decoders and Refl ect & Reset notes. This book doesn't push inspiration. It invites honesty. That distinction makes all the difference.
Keri Jaehnig | Founder & CEO, Idea Girl Media

Funny, raw, and unexpectedly wise. Bonner has a way of pulling something universal out of her very specific story. Starting over doesn't feel dramatic here. It feels human.
Alex Melen | Co-Founder, SmartSites

Reinvention rarely looks the way people expect. It's repetitive, uncomfortable, and usually happens in small steps no one else sees. *Trail & Error* leans into that reality and gets it right.
Brandon Blewett | Author, *How to Avoid Strangers on Airplanes*

The prose is clean, vivid and consistently intentional. There's emotional intelligence woven throughout, but it never turns into instruction. Throughout the book you feel accompanied and guided, not lectured.
Sharmyn Powell | Director, Eastern Caribbean Central Bank

The humor catches your attention first. The heart keeps you there. This memoir never slips into self-help territory, even though it gently shifts your perspective.
Takehito Yokoo | CEO, Jozen Power LLC

Sometimes survival looks ordinary and slightly chaotic. Loading a kayak in the rain. Getting lost. Trying again. This book understands that small acts of courage matter. A fascinating read!**Dr. Rahul Prasad | Physicist, Philanthropist and Adventurer. USA Bestselling author of *Impact Shift: The Art of Pivoting for Meaningful Change* and *Success DNA***

You might finish this book and step outside differently. Not chasing a summit. Just noticing the air. Remembering that moving forward, even slowly, still counts.
Tamara Nall | CEO & Founder, The Leading Niche

Dedication

To my boys, who brought me both the most challenging and most rewarding role—being a mom. You have taught me the value of unconditional love, and you make me proud every day.

To my partner, whom I wasn't expecting but who made me believe in second chances. You helped me find the pieces of myself that were lost and showed me what true partnership is.

To the amazing women who helped me when everything was falling apart. Everyone should have a village like this.

And to all the midlife women who've been playing small or making themselves fit a mold that no longer serves them.

Table of Contents

Introduction

I walked into the restaurant, looking for my dad's longtime girlfriend, Colleen, and my dad's cousin, whom I'd called "Uncle Bob" since I was a child.

The nerves refused to settle. I hadn't seen either of these people in more than a decade. I hadn't seen my dad in person since I graduated from college, and now all I could think about was the message from Uncle Bob telling me my dad was gone. As the restaurant door closed behind me, I had a moment of panic that I wouldn't recognize either of them.

In the span of eighteen months, I buried my father, ended my marriage, stepped into a leadership role I wasn't sure I wanted, and braced myself for a global pandemic—all while pretending I had it under control. I was forty-five, separated, exhausted, and pretending to be fine.

Everyone thought I had it all together. I didn't even know what *together* meant anymore. I was pretending every day: pretending to my boys that we were still a family, even as their dad and I painfully worked at pulling apart seventeen years of marriage; pretending I wasn't terrified about money and going it alone; pretending to the department members I led that I knew what I was doing and could hold all their stress and fear (in addition to my own) as the world flipped upside down in 2020.

And pretending to myself that the resilience I had so carefully cultivated over the last forty years would keep me safe and whole.

Until it didn't.

I didn't have a plan. I just knew I had to move, physically, emotionally, geographically. So I went outside.

Walking around the streets of my neighborhood brought some semblance of peace. I tended to wander at dusk, as night was falling. Longer walks when my boys were with their dad, and their absence felt like a hole. Shorter ones when they were home.

I started by walking, and then moved on to other outdoor activities. Hiking soon felt manageable. Kayaking gave me something to hold onto and the peace of being on the water. I broke in different ways, put the pieces back together, and kept going outside. Nature didn't care about my problems, and every time I looked up at the vast sky, my problems didn't seem so insurmountable.

This book isn't about how I became an outdoor expert (I still trip over rocks on a flat stretch of trail). It's about how getting outside helped me find a new version of myself, one that allows me to grow in ways I never imagined while honoring the versions of me that led to today.

If you're feeling stuck, small, or wondering whether you could make a shift as you enter midlife and beyond, this book is for you.

You don't have to hike the Appalachian Trail or live out of a van to reconnect with your life. You just have to take the first step. Let me tell you what happened when I did.

PART 1
LOST THE MAP

The story I thought I was living collapsed.

Marriage, identity, family—all of it cracked, leaving me disoriented and raw. I wandered in a fog, doing what Gen X kids were trained to do: walk it off, don't cry in public, and pretend you're fine even when you're unraveling.

I carried guilt for my kids, shame for the divorce, and silence where my voice should've been. Vulnerability felt dangerous, so I avoided it. I kept moving through the motions, hoping no one would notice how much had already broken.

This part of the story isn't about adventure. It's about disorientation and denial—about sitting in the rubble of the life I thought I had built, holding shame in one hand and stubbornness in the other.

But even in the fog, there was a spark. Small, quiet, almost invisible. The faintest hint that something different might be possible.

CHAPTER 1

When the Map Disappeared

I walked into the restaurant alone.

The kind with a private dining room tucked behind a sliding barn door—just upscale enough to feel like an event, but not so fancy it felt out of place. The kind of place you book when you're trying to honor someone in a low-key way they would have appreciated.

Photos of my dad were arranged on a side table—fishing trips, trail views, a few candid shots where he wasn't smiling so much as squinting into the sun. There was no formal service. No minister. Just trays of food, soft music, and a room full of people who had once orbited around him.

I wasn't unwelcome. People greeted me warmly. They meant well. But it had been years since I'd seen most of them—decades in some cases—and the conversations had the soft awkwardness of a high school reunion where everyone forgot you transferred out junior year.

The memorial itself was a study in disconnection. I stood in a room full of people who knew parts of my father that I didn't. His longtime girlfriend. My cousins, whom I hadn't seen in decades and who, as it turned out, had been much closer to him than I ever was. The whole thing had the vibe of being the understudy at someone else's funeral. I made small talk, accepted condolences, and watched as people traded stories about a man I only partially recognized.

Someone asked, "Where's your husband?" Another added, "Did the kids come with you?"

I smiled and said, "They couldn't make it," which was technically true and emotionally evasive.

What I didn't say: *We're getting divorced. The kids are home. Everything just… fell apart, and I'm navigating the fallout alone.*

There was no eulogy. No slideshow. But there was a bill.

I had paid for the cremation. My dad's partner didn't have the resources, and someone had to step in. I also covered half the food for the memorial when I saw that my cousin was going to pay for it. No one asked me to, exactly. It just fell to me—because I could, because I knew how to organize things, because I was his daughter.

It was a strange thing, grieving someone you hadn't really known in years. Being responsible without being emotionally connected. Present but slightly out of place. Like showing up to a role you hadn't auditioned for, only to find your name on the program anyway.

All of it left me with a strange, drifting sense of being adjacent to my own family history—close enough to touch, but not rooted inside it. That feeling followed me as we moved from the memorial to the bridge. There wasn't much ceremony, just a quiet shift in where we stood and what came next.

Then came the ashes. As we worked to remove the cover, memories flickered through my mind like quick cut scenes. He taught me how to fish and sail. Wearing the Santa suit he inherited from my grandfather, he waved to passing cars from the pedestrian bridge every Christmas Eve. Scuffing the soles of my brand-new heels so I wouldn't slip at my first formal. Volunteering to chaperone our all-night senior party. Small moments, all of them, but together they told the truth of who he was. He wasn't perfect. But he showed up.

We scattered them off a small bridge overlooking the water near one of his favorite hiking trails. I encouraged his girlfriend and my cousin (my dad's goddaughter) to take the lead, while I stood quietly to the side. The moment was meant to be solemn, but, of course, life had other plans. A gust of wind hit at just the wrong moment, and some of his ashes didn't scatter so much as…cling to the bridge. We had to brush them off.

Sorry, Dad.

He was the master of the Irish goodbye, so he would have been mortified that part of him stuck around.

The Geography of Goodbye

The whole day carried the same uneasy echo—present, but not anchored. Every stop, from the memorial to the bridge, kept reminding me how often I'd been orbiting instead of belonging. That feeling was still with me when I walked into my cousin's rental that evening, a gathering of my uncle's side of the family I hadn't seen in years.

She meant well, hosting with her easy warmth and endless snacks, but walking through that door felt like time travel to a life I'd never actually lived. There were cousins I hadn't seen in decades, significant others, teenagers, and young adults I'd never heard of. Everyone seemed to belong to a shared history I'd missed.

I stood there, surrounded by people whose stories should have been mine to know, and felt the hollow outline of a family I'd lost long before they'd gathered. My parents' divorce had quietly split the map of my childhood, carving out whole branches of family I never really got to know in adulthood. Standing there, surrounded by people who felt both familiar and foreign, I felt the outline of that loss more sharply than I had in years. And now, as my own marriage frayed at the seams, I recognized the cruel symmetry of it. Divorce doesn't just separate two people; it redraws every boundary around them.

That evening, while everyone swapped stories and shared pictures, and laughter filled the kitchen, I realized something I'd been avoiding: when this was all over, I wouldn't just be losing a husband. I'd be losing his family too—the ones who'd once felt like mine. The group texts, the holidays, the casual ease of belonging. All of it would go.

So I smiled through the weekend, hugged the cousins I barely knew, and tucked the ache somewhere quiet. But the realization stayed: every ending multiplies the losses you didn't think to count. Some of what you lose isn't the person—it's the orbit that once made you feel like you had a place.

Grief Logistics as Landmines

The logistics were the part that really knocked me off balance.

Flights, death certificates, vague discussions about obituaries that I wasn't asked to write. Trying to figure out who needed what paperwork, and when. The aftermath of a loss doesn't follow a checklist; it's a minefield of unexpected emotions. Every email or phone call was a chance for grief to sneak in sideways—usually when I least expected it.

There was no estate to manage, at least not involving me. Nothing was left to me in any official way. I wasn't offered anything from the house. I wasn't asked to help close out accounts or sort through belongings. I was a daughter by title, not by task.

I did make one call that mattered: to my dad's former business partner in Germany. They hadn't spoken in years, but I felt like he should hear the news from someone who knew him. The conversation was brief, respectful, and surprisingly tender. It was one of the few moments in that whole stretch of time that felt human instead of procedural.

Around the same time, I got an email from a distant cousin in Sweden. She'd been writing letters back and forth with my dad for years—actual handwritten letters, the kind with stamps and envelopes and everything. She shared a few things he'd told her, little glimpses of his life and thoughts. I didn't know how to respond. It was kind. Thoughtful. Also deeply strange to learn about pieces of my father from a woman I hadn't known existed.

But that was the theme of the week: other people knew him in ways I didn't. Maybe in ways I never could have.

The Night Before the Hike

That night, after the memorial, I lay in a hotel bed that felt both too big and too unfamiliar. I hadn't cried. Not really. I hadn't slept much either. Just lay there staring at the popcorn ceiling, my brain playing a slow, silent slideshow of everything I didn't say that day.

I'd gotten through the awkward conversations. I'd paid my half of the catering bill. I'd nodded politely as people shared stories about a man who was their friend, their cousin, their neighbor. It wasn't that I didn't recognize him in their memories. It's that I barely recognized myself in the room.

The quiet was heavy—not peaceful, but weighted. The kind of quiet where your thoughts get louder because they know no one's going to interrupt.

I didn't journal. I didn't call anyone. I just stared at the ceiling and felt… blank.

And then, almost without thinking, I Googled hiking trails nearby.

It wasn't some grand metaphor. I wasn't chasing healing or clarity or peace. I just wanted out. Out of the hotel. Out of the grief performance. Out of the person I'd been pretending to be for months.

I found a short trail not far from the memorial site—something my dad had liked. I remembered him mentioning it once, or maybe it had shown up in one of the photos. I set the alarm on my phone and rolled over, unsure if I'd actually go.

But something in me already had.

The Hike

The next morning, I laced up my sneakers—hardly trail-appropriate, but they'd have to do. I filled a water bottle from the bathroom sink, grabbed a granola bar from my bag, and drove out to the trailhead with the kind of numb determination usually reserved for DMV visits.

There weren't many cars in the lot. A few early risers were unloading trekking poles. A lone trail runner was stretching next to his Subaru. I tucked my keys in my jacket pocket and started walking— head down, no plan, no playlist, just me and the cold morning air.

The trail wound gradually upward, then dipped into quiet, wooded ravines. The smell of wet leaves and pine hit first—sharp and earthy. Eventually, the sound of water began to rise beneath the birdsong. I followed the curve of the path and came to the first of several waterfalls.

They weren't enormous, but they were beautiful. Ribbons of water tumbling over rocks, framed by moss and morning light. The kind of view that doesn't try too hard, just *is*.

I knew these were trails my dad had taken. He'd mentioned them in passing once—before the distance had grown too wide for casual stories. Long ago, he used to hike them with Shadow, the black Lab he got in the divorce. I'd loved that dog.

I stood there longer than I meant to. Not crying. Not reflecting. Just *there*. The sound of the falls, the cold seeping into my sleeves, the ache in my legs—all of it reminded me that I was still alive. Still moving.

There was no grand epiphany. No dramatic breakthrough. But there was space. And breath. And something just shy of peace.

I wasn't looking for healing. I was just trying to survive the weekend. But something about that walk stayed with me.

Maybe that was the first flicker—the idea that movement might be the only way through, that grief could be quiet and still count, that solitude wasn't the same as loneliness.

I didn't know it yet, but the woman who hiked out of those woods was not quite the same as the one who'd walked in. And maybe that was the point—the trail didn't fix anything, but it gave me a way to keep going.

CHAPTER 2

Marriage in Slow Collapse

We didn't fall apart all at once. There was no big fight, no dramatic exit, nothing you could point to and say, *there—that's where it broke.*

It was quieter than that. Quieter, and somehow heavier.

Months before my father died—before the pandemic, before the real unraveling—we were already living separate lives. He was working a contract job four hours away, home only every other weekend. At first, it felt manageable. Temporary. We both knew how to juggle calendars and kid schedules. I'd grown used to carrying more than my share, the weight settling in so gradually I barely noticed it anymore.

But the space between visits started to feel like more than just physical distance. When he was home, he wasn't really *here.* Conversations became logistics—groceries, repairs, bills, updates about the kids. Efficient. Polite. Friendly.

And completely disconnected.

There was a night, not long before my dad died, when we sat across from each other at the dinner table, and I realized I hadn't touched him in months. Not in anger. Just... hadn't. The silence wasn't tense or dramatic. It was just there, settling between us like dust.

Looking back, that might've been the moment I stopped pretending everything was fine. Or maybe it was the moment I realized I already had.

The Quiet Collapse

People talk about relationships ending in fire. Ours ended in quiet—thin layers of detachment building until there was nothing left to reach for.

Not all at once. Just gradually, in the kind of quiet that fills the space between people who've stopped being curious about each other. The conversations grew shorter. The touchpoints became fewer. The emotional check-ins—nonexistent.

I kept trying, kept showing up, kept doing the emotional work to hold together a marriage on life support. But it took more and more of me just to function. Every interaction felt like a negotiation.

Some nights we went to bed without speaking—not out of anger, but because there was nothing left to say.

We hadn't stopped loving each other. We just stopped reaching for each other. And in that space between the reach and the retreat, the marriage dissolved.

Grieving Alone

By the time my father died, the unraveling was impossible to ignore. We hadn't split yet—not officially—but the decision was already lodged between us like humidity before a storm. So when I flew home for the memorial, I went alone. And it felt strangely familiar.

I was back in one of the places that shaped my childhood, remembering the summers at the family cabin where my dad taught me to fish and we spent long days swimming, reading, and wandering the shoreline. And yet, standing in that room full of people who knew parts of my father I never did, answering polite questions about where my husband was, giving half-smiles that said please don't ask—it echoed the same quiet isolation that had seeped into my marriage. Different losses, but the same hollow feeling. The same sense of being beside your own life instead of inside it.

I was grieving one man while slowly unspooling myself from another. And in both places–in the marriage and at the memorial–I was already grieving alone. And I realized that ending my marriage meant letting go of a partnership I had already stopped leaning on. Not because it had held me so well, but because I had learned not to ask it to. I had been carrying most things myself for a long time, careful about what I showed, careful about what I needed.

What I missed wasn't comfort. It was the idea that I could have expected it. The way marriage is supposed to mean someone stands beside you, even when in practice, you've been standing on your own.

At the memorial, the absence was suddenly visible. Not just to me, but to everyone else. And I understood that I wasn't newly alone. I was finally seeing how long I had already been.

The Long Negotiation with Yourself

Before the decision, there was the negotiation.

Not with him. With myself.

I told myself we were just in a rough patch. That it was the travel schedule, the stress, the kids, and the fatigue of midlife, marriage, and multitasking. I told myself that all marriages go through dry spells. I told myself to be patient, to be grateful, to give it time.

I got really good at pretending things were fine. At rewriting the story in real time so it sounded better in my head. So it sounded like something I could stay in.

But the truth was harder to ignore.

I stopped asking for what I needed—not out of resentment, but out of resignation. I already knew the answer would be a blank stare, a dismissive shrug, or a deflection—sometimes nothing at all. And that kind of silence chips away at you. It makes you smaller, quieter, and more accommodating. Until one day, you realize you don't recognize the version of yourself you've become to keep the peace.

I wanted to stay. I wanted to fix it. I wanted to protect the kids from the pain of watching their parents fall apart. But I also knew: Sometimes, staying for others means leaving yourself behind.

And the longer I stayed, the further I drifted from the woman I was trying to get back to. It wasn't one big moment. It was a hundred small ones. Sitting in the car longer than I needed to after running errands. Breathing more easily when I was alone than when I was in my own home.

Those moments added up to a truth I couldn't unknow:

This marriage wasn't broken because we fought. It was broken because we stopped trying.

The Truth You Can't Unknow

There's a specific kind of grief that comes from ending something you spent years building. Not because it exploded—but because it wore down to dust.

I wasn't leaving because I stopped caring. I was leaving because I'd spent too long caring alone.

Once we made the decision to separate, there was no big release. No dramatic walkout or cathartic shouting match. Just paperwork and calendars and a quiet, mutual understanding that we'd both done what we could—and that it hadn't been enough.

Grief shows up in unexpected moments—when you're folding laundry, loading the dishwasher, or reaching for your phone to share something.

The grief wasn't just for the marriage. It was for the version of me who tried so hard to make it work, who swallowed needs, downplayed disappointments, and called it a compromise. The version of me who stayed long after she knew she was gone.

Losing my dad, ending my marriage, and trying to hold my professional life together all happened in the same season. And in a way, it made sense. Everything that wasn't sustainable finally collapsed under the weight of being unsaid.

I didn't know what came next.

But I knew I couldn't keep carrying the life I had built.

And maybe, just maybe, that wasn't the worst thing.

CHAPTER 3

Chaos and the Myth of Capable

When I interviewed for the department chair position in April 2020, the world was already upside down. No conference room, no handshakes, no eye contact—just a blinking Teams cursor and the faint smell of sanitizer.

I remember obsessing over my background—not because I cared, but because it was something I could control. I shifted a stack of books into frame and moved the pile of bills out of sight, then played with various artificial backgrounds before abandoning another potential tech element that could backfire.

Someone's dog barked through a policy question. Someone else froze mid-sentence for a full ten seconds, their face pixelated in mid-thought. I nodded and smiled like it was all normal, like I wasn't silently praying the Wi-Fi would hold or that my kids wouldn't start a screaming match during the closing question.

"Tell us how you approach leadership in times of uncertainty," someone asked with a completely straight face.

I almost laughed.

To be fair, the job itself wasn't a surprise. I knew the responsibilities. I had ideas. A vision, even. But it's one thing to imagine leadership in theory and quite another to start that leadership in the middle of a once-in-a-century crisis, grieving a parent, and quietly navigating the unraveling of your marriage—all while trying to figure out what day it was.

Of course, in April 2020, we didn't know that it was a once-in-a-century pandemic. As I officially stepped into the role in August, the challenges I faced became even more pronounced.

People First, But Not Me

I officially stepped into the role in August, at a time when the only certainty was that everything could change by next Tuesday. There were no welcome bagels or "how can I support you?" drop-ins from colleagues. Just an inbox full of policy memos and a department full of faculty waiting for someone—me—to know what to do next.

So I did what I always did. I showed up.

I set the tone early: people first. I said it in emails. I said it in meetings. I meant it. I wanted to be the kind of leader who didn't just enforce rules but listened, responded, and adjusted. Someone who understood that people were scared, tired, stretched thin—and needed grace more than ever.

And I tried. I really did. I checked in on faculty. I offered flexibility. I scheduled meetings around kids' Zoom classes and never asked anyone to turn on their cameras. I sent out weekly updates with bullet points and compassion.

But while I was making space for everyone else, I left none for myself.

There wasn't time. Or rather, there wasn't permission—from the job, from the institution, from me. I was the one expected to hold it all together. And if I broke down, who exactly was supposed to pick up the pieces?

So I kept the meetings moving, even when I felt like I might fall apart mid-agenda. I hit "send" on polished updates at 9:48 p.m. after scrubbing the day's panic out of my draft folder. I told everyone else to take breaks. I forgot to eat lunch for a week.

People first.

Just not this person.

Leadership Without a Lifeline

Leading during the pandemic wasn't just hard—it was disorienting.

There was no road map. No margin for error. Just a carousel of pivots and policy updates, none of which came with enough information, clarity, or lead time. One day I was reviewing enrollment projections, and the next I was interpreting CDC guidelines and fielding questions about classroom ventilation systems like I had a background in epidemiology.

The university was scrambling. Everyone was. But when you're in a leadership role, you don't get to show that. You have to translate chaos into direction. You have to be the calm voice on the call while internally screaming, *I don't know either.*

My inbox became a collection of quiet panic—faculty asking for guidance, support, certainty I didn't have. Students writing with real, heartbreaking needs. Administrators forwarding policy changes with subject lines like "please review ASAP." No one was malicious. But no one was looking out for me, either.

There were days I answered emails from the bathroom floor because it was the only place I could close a door. Days I sat at my desk long after the boys were asleep, trying to draft reassuring messages while feeling anything but reassured. I remember one evening staring at a half-written email for nearly an hour, too depleted to decide whether to delete it or hit send. Moments like that made it painfully clear: I was carrying everyone else's fear with nowhere to put my own.

At home, things weren't any better. I was co-parenting through a divorce, navigating remote classes, disrupted routines, and the tense, endless conversations about who had the kids when and what counted as "safe." It felt like running a household, a classroom, and a crisis center at the same time. I was also still fielding the emotional fallout of losing my dad, an emotional fallout that was unpredictable given our adult relationship. There was no time to feel anything. Just a schedule to maintain and a professional mask to keep adjusting.

The irony was sharp: I was surrounded by people—colleagues, students, family—and yet the sense of solitude was overwhelming. That pressure to stay steady for everyone else didn't just exhaust me—it pushed me further into myself, reinforcing the same isolation I felt in every other part of my life.

There's a particular kind of isolation that comes with being the one everyone assumes has it handled. You become the container for everyone else's uncertainty. And you stop noticing how much you're spilling.

When Capable Starts to Cost Too Much

It got me through meetings and hard conversations, through months where my world was either on fire or held together with duct tape. It gave me a role—someone who could handle it—when everything else felt uncertain.

Being capable kept me afloat, but it also kept me from asking for help.

My days started with coffee and ended with emails I couldn't remember sending. Some mornings, I woke with my jaw clenched so tight it took half the morning for the ache to fade. The kids were doing remote school. My internal monologue was 90 percent logistics and 10 percent, is this my life now?

And yet I kept going. Because when people see you as capable, they stop asking if you're okay. Eventually, you stop asking yourself.

There's a particular weight to being the person who keeps it together. You get good at hiding the cracks. You learn to mute Zoom just in time to take a breath—or scream into a pillow. You become so practiced at calm that even you start to believe it.

Behind the emails and policies and check-ins, I was slowly disappearing. My body was exhausted. My mind was fraying. I could only find myself alone in the woods or locked in the bathroom with the faucet running. I didn't tell anyone how bad it had gotten. I didn't want to break the illusion or scare anyone. Mostly, I didn't want to admit it to myself.

But hairline fractures were spreading. Not all at once, not dramatic—just enough to know this version of me couldn't keep going much longer.

What I didn't understand then was that my ability to manage chaos wasn't strength; it was survival. And survival has an expiration date.

I didn't know what waited on the other side. I only suspected—hoped—that it might be something freer.

CHAPTER 4

Pandemic Pressure Cooker

In March 2020, the world hit pause. And then it imploded.

One day, I was juggling parenting, grief, and a full workload with the usual level of caffeine and denial. Next, my kids were home indefinitely, my calendar had turned into a graveyard of canceled meetings, and I was wiping down boxes of cereal with Clorox wipes like that might actually save us.

We were nearly a year into the divorce decision without a lot of movement. I was still picking through the emotional rubble of when the pandemic arrived like a cosmic punchline: *Oh, you thought you were overwhelmed already? Cute.*

Schools closed. Work went remote. Everyone started talking about "pivoting," "flattening the curve," and "the new normal," while I tried to figure out how to become a homeschool teacher, tech support, and emotional anchor—all from the same spot at the kitchen table.

There was no real panic at first. Just a kind of stunned, low-grade chaos. Group texts buzzing with toilet paper shortages. Team channels full of hastily uploaded syllabi. The news refreshed every few minutes, each headline worse than the last.

I wasn't a department chair yet. That would come later. But already, I was the one holding everything together—for my kids, my students, myself.

I hadn't had time to process the end of my marriage. I was still trying to bring it to a conclusion, with lawyers and spreadsheets.

And now I had no room to process anything at all. Just a full house, a fractured heart, and a calendar that suddenly meant nothing.

And the place I expected to be my refuge wasn't one.

The Home Front Wasn't Exactly a Sanctuary

There's a lie we tell ourselves when things outside our sphere get hard: *At least home is a refuge.*

Except, sometimes it's not.

By April, we were all home, all the time. My kids were trying to adjust to remote school, which mostly meant glitchy logins, forgotten passwords, and teachers valiantly narrating over a sea of muted microphones. I was running triage on their schoolwork while also answering work emails and figuring out how to explain a global pandemic to two children without terrifying them.

There were moments it felt comical, in a sitcom-tragic sort of way. I'd finally get everyone settled–laptops charged, links working, cereal bowls cleared–only for someone to unplug the router mid-Zoom call or yell "MOM" loud enough to startle me during a faculty meeting.

We were all doing our best. And we were all fraying.

I was grieving, divorcing, and trying to stay functional, and now I also had to play IT support and cafeteria worker while keeping the house from looking like a laundry bomb had gone off. There was no room to think, no silence to retreat into. There was nowhere to go to escape.

I missed the simple act of closing a door and knowing no one needed anything from me on the other side. I missed knowing what day it was. I missed not feeling like I was one printer jam away from full collapse.

My soon-to-be ex was now in the same city, because we were trading the kids back and forth every week. We orbited the same space like indifferent satellites–coexisting but not connecting.

And still, I smiled for the kids. I ordered craft kits. I bought an Insta Pot like the rest of the internet. I tried so hard to make it feel normal, even when nothing was.

Because when home stops being a sanctuary, you do what women have always done: you try to make it one anyway.

A Silver Lining, Right There in the Mess

And yet–somewhere in the chaos, there was softness.

Without carpools and morning commutes and weekend obligations, there was finally… time.

Time to build epic LEGO cities.

Time to watch movies curled up under one blanket.

Time to linger over microwave mac and cheese and giggle over nothing at all.

Time for the boys to show me their latest Minecraft builds while talking over each other in that excited way only twins can. Time to pause in the middle of a school day and laugh about the absurdity of taking band via video recordings of "Hot Cross Buns."

We had nowhere to be. And for the first time in years, I wasn't rushing them out the door or barking at them to get shoes on. The world had stopped spinning, and for all its horror and uncertainty, it gave us this one strange gift: uninterrupted togetherness.

We made popcorn at 2 p.m.

We built blanket forts in the living room.

We celebrated virtual Halloween with treat buckets, movies, and cozy pajamas.

We went on neighborhood walks to the lake to see if we could spy the two herons that called it home. We ate breakfast for dinner for no reason—pancakes shaped like whatever the boys requested, most of them unrecognizable but enthusiastically eaten anyway.

It wasn't perfect. I was still grieving the end of a seventeen-year marriage. Still raw. Still checking emails between puzzles and feeling guilty about every ball I dropped. But the time with my kids was real in a way that most of life hadn't been for a while.

And in the quiet moments—when the screens were off and the laughter had faded into soft bedtime breathing—I noticed something else.

It was easier to breathe when he wasn't in the room.

There was a lightness to the space he left behind. An absence that didn't ache.

A version of peace I hadn't known I was craving.

I didn't know what the future would look like yet. But I knew this: Even here, in the middle of a global breakdown, some part of me felt steadier than it had in a long time.

Institutional Chaos Meets Personal Crisis

While I was navigating remote school and virtual meetings, the university was in full-on panic mode. Guidelines changed weekly. Policies shifted daily. No one knew what fall would look like, but everyone expected answers—and soon.

In the middle of that mess, I was interviewing for the department chair position. On Teams, of course. Because why not add *"audition for a leadership role"* to a grief-and-divorce apocalypse?

It was April 2020. I had one foot in a dissolving marriage, one foot in institutional chaos, and no spare limbs to hold anything steady. And yet… I said yes. I told myself it was the right step, professionally. That leadership was the logical next move. That I needed something to anchor me.

What I didn't say out loud was that I also needed to prove I could still do hard things. That I wasn't crumbling, even though I was.

Meanwhile, the divorce—though emotionally quiet—was dragging like a rock tied to my ankle. It wasn't overly contentious, just impossibly stuck. I had to sue him just to get the clock started. What should have taken months stretched into more than a year. It drained money I didn't have and energy I couldn't spare.

There were no blowups, no dramatic courtroom scenes—just endless paperwork and silence, punctuated by legal fees and waiting.

All of that was happening behind the scenes while, on camera, I was the calm presence in a sea of blinking boxes. A reliable voice on the department's weekly emails. The person who read the memos, translated the policies, and made the plans. The person who knew what to do.

Except I didn't. I was guessing. I was tired. I was grieving a parent, a partner, and a version of myself I no longer recognized.

And no one really saw it. Because I didn't let them.

The Slow Burn of Isolation and Overwhelm

There wasn't one big breaking point. No dramatic collapse. Just a thousand tiny ones.

A spilled cup of coffee that made me cry.

An unanswered text that echoed like rejection.

The printer refusing to work—for the fourth time that week—and me standing in front of it, shaking with frustration, like it was personally conspiring against me.

I wasn't just tired. I was eroded.

Grief doesn't tap you on the shoulder and say, *Hey, it's time to cry now.* It sneaks in during the downtime—except there wasn't any downtime. I was parenting full-time, managing a department remotely, and trying to finalize a divorce that wouldn't end.

Support systems frayed. Friends were also struggling. Everyone was maxed out. There was no space to vent, no girls' night out, no comforting touch on the shoulder. Just texts we were too exhausted to answer and phone calls we let ring out.

Even when I reached for connection, it felt distant. Like everyone was underwater, waving but unable to speak.

And then there was the loneliness that came from being seen as "capable." When you're the one who keeps it together, people stop checking in. They assume you've got it handled. And eventually, so do you.

So when something broke—or I did—I just picked it up, quietly, and kept moving.

Burnout, But Make It Existential

By the end of 2020, I wasn't just burned out—I was hollowed out.

Every piece of me had been spoken for: by my kids, by my job, by the legal process crawling toward divorce, by the version of myself I kept trying to perform even though I no longer recognized her.

I didn't have the luxury of falling apart. But that didn't mean I was intact.

There's a strange loneliness in being the person everyone depends on. You get so used to absorbing everyone else's stress, showing up with a plan, holding space, making it work—that you forget you were never meant to do it all alone.

But I had. For months. Years, really. And something inside me had finally gone quiet.

Not in a peaceful way. In a *numb* way.

And still, I kept going.

Because that's what capable women do.

But somewhere deep in the mess of that year, a truth began to take root—quietly, stubbornly: If the world could fall apart overnight, then maybe I could finally let go of the version of me who thought she had to hold it all together.

CHAPTER 5

What Stayed When Everything Else Fell Apart

I avoided vulnerability like the plague. One therapist once told me I threw off trauma like no one he'd ever seen. At the time, I took it as a compliment.

(Spoiler: it was not.)

I don't do introspection well. I don't cry at movies. I rarely know what I'm feeling in real time. Some of that is me. Much of it is Gen X.

We came of age as "latchkey kids." We were sent home after school unsupervised, expected to fend for ourselves emotionally and practically. The hidden cost of early independence was always having to patch your own emotional wounds.

Mental health was taboo. Depression and anxiety were for "real" trauma, not for everyday unraveling. We inherited a culture that told us to "tough it out," to never let the internal leak into public view.

We were feral in the most functional way. Independent, sarcastic, emotionally constipated. And we were expected to figure it out, walk it off, and never, under any circumstances, make a big deal out of it.

So no, I didn't wake up one day and say, *You know what I need? A journey of radical self-discovery.*

What I had was something quieter. A low-grade ache. A bone-deep knowing that something inside me was *wrong*. Not broken, just misaligned. Like I'd stayed too long in someone else's life, and the seams were finally giving way.

What Let Go of Me (Before I Let Go of It)

I didn't decide to let everything go. Not consciously.

It just started falling off me. Piece by piece.

The marriage.

The performative smiling.

The belief that holding it together made me strong.

I didn't wake up one morning and say, *I'm done performing.* I just ran out of energy to keep it up. Like a costume that finally stopped fitting—but not in a dramatic, rip-it-off moment. More like realizing one sleeve is torn, and the zipper's stuck, and honestly, you don't even like the damn thing anymore.

Some things I let go of willingly.

Others let go of me.

And in the middle of that shedding, I realized I wasn't just losing a marriage or a role—I was losing the version of myself I'd been holding together for years.

It left me feeling strangely untethered, like someone who'd stepped out of a life mid-scene and wasn't sure what lines she was supposed to deliver next.

The illusion of control was one of the first to go.

So was the fantasy that once the divorce was final, things would feel resolved.

They didn't.

They felt… emptier.

But not in a bad way. In a *quiet* way.

Like when the party finally ends, everyone goes home, and you can hear your own breath again.

It wasn't just the big things that fell away. It was the little ones, too:

- Responding to every work email as if it were an Olympic event
- Smiling through conversations I had no energy for
- Pretending I wasn't tired when I'd been tired for years

All of that started slipping. And at first, I tried to catch it. Patch it. Pick it back up.

But eventually, I just let it fall.

Pretending was heavier than telling the truth.

And I was so, so tired.

What Stayed—Even When Everything Else Didn't

Not everything broke.

Some things held. Some things held *me*.

My kids, for one. They were still there, still asking for snacks, still building LEGO villages with wild architectural ambition and no regard for gravity.

We watched movies, the same ones on repeat. We made microwave popcorn and fell asleep on the couch. Sometimes they'd snuggle into me while watching a movie, and for just a second, I'd forget that everything else had changed.

Those moments weren't big. They weren't the kind people write essays about. But they were *mine*. And they reminded me that not everything had to be falling apart.

My sense of humor stuck around, too.

Dry. Sharp. A little darker than before, maybe—but intact.

Even when I felt like I'd lost track of who I was, the part of me that could make someone laugh? Still there.

Sarcasm is a survival tool. Especially when the alternative is crying in front of your children because the check engine light is on again.

And then there was movement.

At first, I didn't call it that. I just needed to get outside. To breathe something that wasn't recycled air and fluorescent light.

I didn't have a fitness tracker or a hiking plan. I wasn't "getting my steps in."

I just wanted space.

Quiet.

I wanted to be somewhere that didn't expect anything from me.

Where I didn't have to be "Chair" or "Mom" or "Person Who Has Her Shit Together."

Just… me. Or whoever I was now. Or might become.

That pull—to put one foot in front of the other—wasn't about escape. It was something closer to return.

To myself. Or at least to *something* that wasn't trying to hold me hostage.

The First Craving for Space

It didn't feel like a breakthrough.

It felt like I couldn't breathe.

The morning after my kids went to their dad's for the week, I woke up in the quietest house I'd ever slept in. No footsteps. No doors. No one asking what's for breakfast. The silence pressed against the walls until even the refrigerator hum sounded too loud.

No kids. No emails. No one needing anything from me.

Nothing on the schedule. Nothing to fix.

Just air–and I didn't know what to do with it.

So I laced up my boots and left.

No grand plan, no gear checklist. Just a city trail I'd meant to try for years, a ribbon of green tucked between traffic and water.

I wasn't trying to heal. I wasn't trying to process anything.

I was just walking.

And somewhere between the second creek bed and the steep climb back up, my body remembered what ease felt like. My shoulders dropped. My breath deepened. The pinball machine in my brain–always ricocheting between logistics, guilt, and to-do lists–finally went quiet.

It wasn't dramatic.

It was just still.

No demands. No masks. No performance.

Just me, moving through air that didn't expect me to be anyone but a woman in boots, with a pack and an open afternoon.

I didn't call it freedom then.

But it was the first time I'd felt untethered from the noise.

Identity in the Rubble

Without the marriage, without the routines, without the nonstop performing, I wasn't sure who I was anymore.

I had always defined myself by my roles: professor, partner, parent, competent fixer of all things. When those structures cracked–or dissolved entirely–I expected to feel liberated.

Instead, I just felt… untethered.

I didn't miss the conflict. I didn't miss the pretending.

But I also didn't know how to be a version of myself without the scaffolding I'd spent decades constructing.

It was like walking through the shell of a house after a fire. You're grateful to be alive, but where the hell do you even start?

I remember the day I took my rings off for good and couldn't understand why he continued to wear his. He took the boys to church–the first time in a long while–and later told me he hadn't mentioned the divorce to anyone. Pretending to still be married fit his narrative, but not mine.

There were moments of quiet relief–when I didn't have to negotiate for space, when I didn't have to mute my needs to keep the peace.

But there was grief, too. Grief for the vision I'd carried of how things were supposed to go. For the woman I thought I was building a life for. For the version of me that believed working harder would eventually fix everything.

The house felt too big, too quiet, that first week the kids weren't with me. And then it hit me: I would only see half the rest of their childhood. Half the pictures, half the memories. They would go on vacations I didn't plan, visit family that was no longer mine.

The identity loss wasn't neat. It wasn't a clean break or a glossy reinvention. It was messy and lingering.

But within that discomfort, I started noticing something I hadn't had in years: space.

Not just physical space, but mental space.

Room to breathe, to not be productive, to not be needed.

I still didn't know who I was becoming.

But I was starting to believe that question was worth sitting with.

The Myth of Reinvention

I didn't set out to reinvent myself.

There was no dramatic declaration, no vision board, no phoenix-rising moment scored by Fleetwood Mac.

I just wanted to stop crying in grocery store parking lots.

Turns out, that was a pretty good place to start.

The world had handed me a pile of rubble and no map. And I was just beginning to figure out how to sift through it.

Reinvention sounds like a choice. Like something you do on purpose, with confidence and matching stationery.

This wasn't that.

This was letting go of the person I thought I had to be.

This was breathing again, even if I still felt like I was underwater.

This was noticing—just barely—that something new might be possible.

Eventually.

Even if I didn't know who I was becoming yet, I knew she wouldn't settle for what I had survived.

And that was enough. For now.

Part 1 Conclusion: Lost the Map

The map didn't reappear. I just learned to move without it.

After the memorial and the emails and the polite conversations with people who knew a version of my father I didn't, I did the only thing that made sense: I walked. Not toward an answer—toward air. A short trail. A bench that didn't require small talk. I wasn't brave. I was desperate. But desperation counts.

Nothing has been resolved out there. The marriage was still ending. The paperwork still waited. My jaw would still lock in the mornings. But in the quiet—water over rock, birds stitching sound through trees—I felt something I hadn't felt in months: room. A pocket of space big enough to hear my own breath.

Part 1 ends here, with rubble still everywhere and a tiny spark refusing to go out. I'm not ready for epics. I'm barely ready for honest sentences. But I can do this: put one foot in front of the other, say one small yes, and see if movement can carry what standing still could not.

Turn the page. The fog doesn't lift all at once. It thins as you walk.

PART 2

TRIPPED ON THE TRAILHEAD

Starting over never looks graceful.

When I first stepped outside after my divorce, I wasn't chasing mountaintops or trying to reinvent myself as some backcountry badass. I just needed space. Space to breathe, to think, to feel something other than grief and guilt pressing in on all sides.

The trail called, but not with poetry. More like with sarcasm. Every beginner step felt clumsy: wrong shoes, wrong gear, wrong expectations. I learned quickly that "easy" hikes could still wreck me, blisters could humble me, and REI salespeople had a gift for sparking panic spirals about stealthy mountain lions.

But here's the thing: every stumble was still movement. Every false start counted. And what I couldn't find in boots or bear spray, I found in the people who showed up when I couldn't stand steady on my own.

This part of the story isn't about summits or successes. It's about tripping at the trailhead—messy beginnings, awkward lessons, and the quiet, ordinary friendships that marked the path forward.

CHAPTER 6

The First Craving for Space

I didn't know what I wanted. I only knew it wasn't inside.

After the separation, the house felt too quiet, like someone had sucked the air out. The dishwasher hummed like it was trying to soothe me; the hallway echoed more than it ever had. I'd leave mugs on the counter just to make the kitchen look lived-in. The kids' doors stayed mostly closed—little *Do Not Disturb* signs on a life I used to organize by the minute. The TV droned with some cooking show I wasn't watching, purely so the silence wouldn't press against my ears.

I moved from room to room doing logistics—bills, school forms, work deadlines—while my body buzzed with a restlessness I couldn't name. It was grief, yes, but also something else—a kind of hunger.

I didn't crave company. I didn't crave distraction. I craved air. Trees. Space.

Sometimes the craving was physical—a tightness in my ribs, like my body was running out of room to hold everything I hadn't said. Even breathing felt crowded.

For years, I had lived in the tight orbit of family life. Marriage, kids, career—it all kept me circling a small and predictable universe. When that orbit broke apart, I didn't just lose a partner; I lost the invisible structure that kept me contained. And now here I was, with more quiet than I could stand, and a body practically humming with the need to move.

MINI HOW-TO

5-Sense Reset (When Home Is Too Loudly Quiet)

When everything around you goes still and your brain won't, do this:

Sight: focus on one small thing—light through the blinds, steam from your mug.

Sound: name three things you hear. The fridge hum counts.

Smell: inhale something earthy—coffee, pine candle, house-plant dirt.

Touch: feel the chair, the floor, the air against your skin.

Taste: sip water or tea and actually notice it.

Five senses, five seconds, full stop. You just reminded your nervous system you're safe, just overstimulated.

I couldn't stand another conversation that ended with "You're so strong." Strength was the problem. I didn't want endurance; I wanted ease.

The craving wasn't for adventure. It was for relief.

DECODER

ADVENTURE ≠ RELIEF (KNOW WHAT YOU NEED)
SOMETIMES WE CALL IT "GETTING AWAY," BUT ESCAPE AND RENEWAL AREN'T THE SAME THING.
ADVENTURE WAKES YOU UP; RELIEF CALMS YOU DOWN.
WHEN YOU'RE BURNED OUT, A SUMMIT WON'T FIX IT—BUT A SLOW WALK AND NO AGENDA MIGHT.
KNOW WHAT YOU'RE CRAVING BEFORE YOU PACK THE CAR.

Once upon a time, "adventure" meant family road trips with a trunk full of sports gear or conference travel where I squeezed in a museum between sessions. Those had itineraries, budgets, confirmation numbers–adventure as project management. This felt different. What I wanted now was the opposite of the itinerary. I wanted space to not be in charge of anyone's experience. To not "optimize" a single thing.

Sometimes relief looked like a slow loop around the neighborhood, one foot in front of the other just to prove I could still move forward. I'd pass the same mailbox with peeling paint, smell the sweetness of cut grass braided with hot asphalt, and count cracks in the sidewalk because my brain needed something simple to do.

Even a few minutes outside helped. Studies later confirmed what my body already knew: ten minutes in nature can drop stress hormones and quiet a racing mind. At the time, I just called it breathing.

FIELD NOTES

SOLO WEEK ESSENTIALS

FOR A PRINTABLE PACKING CHECKLIST AND SAFETY REMINDERS, VISIT ROOKIEOUTDOORWOMAN.COM/TRAILANDERROR.

THREE MUST-HAVES FOR A RESTORATIVE SOLO TRIP:

- ONE COMFORT ITEM (RIDICULOUS PAJAMAS COUNT).
- FOOD THAT MAKES YOU HAPPY, NOT VIRTUOUS.
- A PLAN TO DO ABSOLUTELY NOTHING PRODUCTIVE.

THE GOAL ISN'T SURVIVAL–IT'S BREATHING ROOM.

Sometimes it meant pulling into a nearby park, parking the car, and sitting at a sunbaked picnic table, watching a little boy zoom a toy truck through dust while somebody's sunscreen drifted on the breeze. Once, it was a fifteen-minute drive to a scenic over-look where the world opened up into green and sky. I ate drive-thru fries, salt on my fingers, grease on the napkin, and let the view breathe for me. I remember thinking, *You don't have to solve anything up here. Just sit.*

None of it was epic. But all of it mattered.

Permission Slips

That's why National Park Week caught my attention.

Scrolling one evening, I saw the reminder: fee-free entrance on opening day. The thought lodged like an invitation I hadn't known I was waiting for. I wasn't ready for 12-mile hikes or sunrise summits. I barely had the stamina to keep the kids fed and myself upright. But the idea of a low-stakes, no-excuses day to just show up at a park? That I could do.

I later wrote for *Rookie Outdoor Woman*, "If visiting a National Park sounds like something that involves 12-mile hikes, bear-proof canisters, and someone yelling 'Let's summit before sunrise!'– don't worry. That's not what we're doing here." It was a joke, but also a map. I needed an open door, not a finish line.

So I drove to a nearby historic battlefield–paved paths, interpre-tive signs, cannons placed just so. Families clustered around plac-ards while kids clambered on stone walls. A ranger adjusted his flat hat and talked about troop movements as cardinals heckled from the trees. The sun warmed my shoulders. No one needed me to host or translate or make it *fun*. History is often packaged as a family experience, but that day I claimed it solo. I read the plaques out of order. I stood too long under a sycamore, just for the shade. I let the quiet be quiet and felt my chest loosen a notch.

Apparently, my nervous system was smarter than I was–it prescribed sunlight and motion long before I understood the science. Bit by bit, those tiny solo moments revealed something I hadn't noticed: I liked my own company more than I expected.

The Beach

Not long after custody details were decided—but long before the divorce was final—I took a bigger leap.

I booked a week at the beach by myself.

Typing in my credit card for that rental felt rebellious. It might have been the first time I'd gone anywhere alone for that long. No kids. No partner. No one else's schedule to manage. Just me.

The house was nothing fancy—shingled siding, sandy porch steps, the faint salt-and-mildew smell every East Coast rental collects. The furniture was a collage of "previously loved" pieces; six different grandmothers had clearly contributed. But the windows opened to the ocean, and when the sliding door stuck halfway, I left it that way to hear the waves all night.

I had packed a stack of books, determined to read without interruption. They sat unopened on the nightstand, a still life of good intentions. I didn't want words. I wanted water. I dragged a folding chair to the surf line and let the tide act as a metronome for my nervous system. On the first night, I locked the door and stood in the quiet, palms flat against it, waiting for guilt or panic to come. Instead: wave on wave, then my own breath, finally audible.

People asked, "Is it safe to go alone?" A few said, "Must be nice," with a little edge to it. No one ever asked my ex if he was selfish for golfing alone.

Apparently, men need "me time" while women need therapy.

But somehow, a woman booking seven days by the ocean reads like an indictment: *Are you running away? Do you need rescuing?*

Here's the truth: solo time isn't a scandal; it's survival.

That week was part healing, part discovery. I walked until my calves complained. I cried hard and then laughed at myself because the ocean has seen far worse than one midlife woman leaking feelings. Mostly, I listened–for the first time in a long time–to what my own voice sounded like when no one else was in the room.

Like many Gen X women, I was raised to walk it off, not sit with it. Stillness felt suspicious at first, like I was doing something wrong by resting.

It wasn't glamorous. It wasn't a movie montage. But it was a start. Something in me flickered there, between the tides.

MINI HOW-TO

First Solo Hike (Ultra-Low Stakes)

Pick a short, well-marked loop you already know.
Tell one person your plan and check in afterward.
Bring water, snacks, and put your phone on airplane mode.
Hike at a talking pace. Notice the trees, not the miles.
Celebrate afterward–coffee counts as a summit ritual.

The Solo Habit

Once I tasted how restorative alone time could be, I wanted more. Enter the tiny cabin in the woods–one of those little Getaway-style spots with a picture window, a fire ring, and just enough space for me, my thoughts, and too many snacks.

There were plenty of trails nearby, and I, in true rookie fashion, chose a "simple" loop. The trailhead kiosk had a map with cheerful arrows. I took a photo, felt competent, and headed in. Ten minutes later, I stopped noticing blazes because the path felt obvious. Fifteen minutes after that, "obvious" dissolved into four equally convincing directions. My phone service hovered at one bar, the sun slid behind a cloud, and every root on the forest floor conspired to trip me at once.

I did the rookie shuffle–backtracked, second-guessed, circled a big mossy stump twice like it might give directions if I looked earnest enough. My water bottle was half empty because I'd decided one would be "plenty for a short loop." (Narrator: It was not.) I finally forced myself to slow down and look up. There: a faint, reassuring rectangle of paint on a tree I'd blown past. I followed blazes with a new kind of reverence–counting them, checking the next one before I moved on, letting relief unclench my shoulders. I popped back out at the trailhead ninety frazzled minutes later, equal parts proud and annoyed. Lesson learned: the woods will forgive ignorance once. After that, bring humility, water, and a better plan.

Those cabins, those small mistakes, were where I started connecting the dots: being outdoors alone wasn't just possible–it was nourishing.

FIELD NOTES

Easy Wins for New Rookies
Want the outdoors without the logistics?
Join a ranger-led walk–they handle the map; you handle the wonder.
Still homebound? The Park Service streams trails, geysers, and tide pools.
Zero bugs, maximum serotonin.
Full list and links: RookieOutdoorWoman.com/trailanderror.

I have an app that assesses my energy, stress, and health using heart rate variability. It provides a nice visual color cue on my watch so I know where my biorhythms stand. I took before-and-after pics for my colleagues one time—red when I arrived at the mountain, and green when I left.

Forest-bathing studies would later prove it—heart rate down, mood up—but I didn't need the data. I could feel it in my bones. Sometimes I'd notice it halfway through a hike, when my shoulders finally dropped from around my ears without me telling them to.

Small Starts

Braver didn't mean extreme. Most days, my craving for space still looked beautifully ordinary. I collected "permission slips" the way other people collect loyalty points: a flat greenway with a bench at the halfway mark; a ranger walk where someone else did the talking; a virtual "hike" when I couldn't make myself leave the house (yes, I watched a 12-minute YouTube video of waterfalls and counted it; my nervous system agreed). Once, I went to a tree-ID talk and learned exactly three things: oaks, maples, and that I will never confidently identify anything beyond "that's a pine."

These weren't victories anyone else would notice. They were micro-movements. But for me, they were everything. Each time I stepped outside, I felt a little less trapped by my own thoughts.

Researchers call these micro-restorations—tiny hits of calm that add up to real change. Turns out, peace compounds like interest.

After forty, your idea of "fun" shifts. I wasn't chasing "strenuous" anything. That wasn't laziness; it was wisdom. The outdoors didn't care about my fitness tracker or my inbox or whether my pants had zip-off knees like a tactical Transformer. Nature just existed—calmly, quietly—and let me match its pace.

Space as Medicine

Here's what I didn't understand then but know now: craving space is self-preservation. When your inner world is chaotic, your body goes looking for outer calm.

I couldn't always name what I was feeling—grief, guilt, shame. But I could name what I saw: sunlight netted through leaves; clouds herding themselves across a blue field; ripples stitching the surface of a pond. Or waves rolling in, hour after hour, like a metronome for a frayed nervous system.

Later, when I wrote about *Blue Mind*, I learned there's science behind why water steadies us. Marine biologist Wallace J. Nichols uses that term for the calm, lightly focused state people experience near water—our brains quiet, stress hormones dip, and even brief exposure helps reset us. I didn't know the citations at the time. I just knew that, sitting by the ocean or a fountain, I felt a little less like I was unraveling.

Apparently, relief counts as progress.

Those became anchors when everything else felt untethered.

FIELD NOTES

BLUE MIND STARTER
LEARN MORE ABOUT THE CALMING SCIENCE OF WATER—PLUS MY FAVORITE "RESET BY WATER" SPOTS AND A PRINTABLE REFLECTION GUIDE—AT ROOKIEOUTDOORWOMAN.COM/TRAILANDERROR.
UPDATES APPEAR SEASONALLY, BECAUSE SCIENCE AND SANITY ARE BOTH ONGOING PROJECTS.

From Craving to Carrying

I'd love to tell you the craving for space turned me into an instant outdoorswoman—that I laced up boots and strode into a new chapter. That's not what happened.

Instead, I carried snacks. I carried water. I carried a growing awareness that outside helped—even when I had no idea what I was doing.

And slowly, those tiny starts added up. Each short walk, each sit by a lake, each "does five minutes count?" laugh built a quiet sort of confidence. Not the chest-thumping kind. The kind that says: you don't have to be ready. You just have to start.

In those early months, snacks and water were my training wheels— literal fuel for shaky legs and a jumpy mind. I paired them with the other things I carried: coffee with a friend who let me say the hard parts out loud; a sense of humor that kept me from spiraling; a corner of the internet (*hi, Substack*) where I could tell the truth and be met with "same." Piece by piece, I learned to move through the world without gripping the handlebars so tight.

Every small step outside counted. The craving for space cracked me open just enough to move. And once you move, the next question becomes inevitable: *what do you need to bring with you?*

I started outside looking for air; I ended up finding a little room inside myself.

REFLECT & RESET

WHERE DO YOU BREATHE BEST?
NAME ONE PLACE—BEACH, PARK BENCH, FRONT PORCH—THAT LETS YOUR SHOULDERS DROP.
SCHEDULE FIFTEEN MINUTES THERE THIS WEEK. NO AGENDA. NO PHONE TIMER.
JUST SPACE, ON PURPOSE.

CHAPTER 7

Who Let Me Buy All This Gear?

Here's the thing about deciding to "get outside" in midlife: you don't just walk out the door. You spiral into a world of gear. Shoes, packs, poles, sprays, snacks—there's a product for every scenario, and none of them come with a manual that says: *for women who are 47 and figuring it out.* In some ways, the gear choices mirrored everything else—I was learning as I went.

So I did what any rookie does. I guessed. Badly.

Late at night, I scrolled Amazon reviews like they were sacred texts: "Runs small but great ankle support," "Blew out after two hikes," "Saved my life during a surprise hailstorm." By midnight, my cart looked like I was training for Everest and also…a picnic. On weekends, I'd wander into REI and stand frozen between two walls of water filters, reading words like *hollow fiber membrane* as if I understood them.

Sometimes, staring into that fluorescent wilderness, I caught my reflection in a display case—tired, hopeful, absurd. The glow of the laptop or the aisle lights felt like companionship. Somewhere between the reviews and my reflection, I looked both determined and ridiculous.

Everywhere I looked, the marketing voice in my head belonged to a twenty-four-year-old man who sleeps on granite ledges for fun. Decision fatigue set in, and I left with the only things I could commit to: bougie trail snacks and aspirational confidence.

First Steps Into the Wilderness

Before I bought a single "real" item, I tried dragging my kids on a trail. It seemed wholesome—fresh air, memories, maybe a new phase where we discovered we were "outdoorsy" together.

It was, instead, a masterclass in adolescent negotiations.

"How much longer?"
"Why are we even doing this?"
"My feet hurt."
"Do we have Wi-Fi here?"

Mosquitoes orbited like tiny helicopters. One kid dragged a stick that doubled as a sword and a trip hazard. I was already sweating through my shirt, already doubting the plan, and somewhere around minute twenty-seven, I started bargaining with whatever trail spirit governs teen attitudes. The wilderness did not intervene.

Lesson one: Gear doesn't fix bad attitudes. Not theirs, not mine.

My new partner wasn't much help. He loved the outdoors, but not hiking. He could fish all day—patient, happy, sunburned—but a trail? Hard pass. Which meant if I wanted to figure out hiking, I was mostly on my own.

REFLECT & RESET

REFRAME YOUR FALSE START
PICK ONE "FAIL" THAT TAUGHT YOU SOMETHING YOU STILL USE.
WAS IT TIMING? BOUNDARIES? HYDRATION?
THAT'S NOT FAILURE—THAT'S REHEARSAL.

Gen X latchkey muscle memory kicked in. I grew up figuring stuff out without a manual. We grew up improvising dinner and feelings alike. Fine. I'd improvise. And in true Gen X fashion, I assumed I could figure it out as I went. Which brings us to the shoes.

Betrayed by My Own Feet

The first mistake was footwear.

I bought some nice-looking hiking boots online. They looked the part, and I was proud to have something that wasn't sneakers that I could use on the trails. I was all set, right?

Wrong.

Gravel crunched like broken glass underfoot. The path pitched and rolled, roots reaching up like they had opinions about my ankles. Ten minutes in, the hot spots started whispering. Twenty minutes in, they were shouting. By the time I limped back to the car, my socks were welded to raw spots, and my inner monologue had turned into a profanity-laced TED Talk on life choices.

I'd expected discomfort. I hadn't expected the weird mix of shame and pride that comes from hurting yourself trying to heal.

I later wrote it plain: cheap boots will betray you. If you think you can waltz into the woods in whatever was on clearance, I salute your confidence—and hope you enjoy blisters the size of quarters and contemplating your life choices mid-trail. I ended up hobbling out of the woods like a wounded gazelle—only less graceful, with more swearing.

At home, I peeled off socks like biologists performing a delicate specimen reveal, dabbed at the damage, and googled *what is moleskin* while standing on one foot at the bathroom sink. I had assumed boots would make me feel like a hiker. That if I looked the part, maybe I'd be the part. The woods, however, are not fooled by vibes. They are impressed by fit, socks, and humility.

Blisters make excellent teachers. They taught me that gear matters—but not in the way I thought. You don't need the fanciest setup. You need what works.

And in midlife, we've all made "cheap shoe" choices—shortcuts we hoped would save time or money, only to pay double in pain. Boots, it turns out, are a metaphor.

Before my next outing, I went to a quality gear store and got fitted for boots. More expensive, more time, but my feet have thanked me ever since.

Turns out, even mild hikes can lower cortisol and blood pressure—though that day, I think mine spiked in protest.

TRAIL TRUTH

CHEAP BOOTS ARE EXPENSIVE
COMFORT COSTS LESS THAN REGRET.

OUTDOOR EFFECT

HIKING AS RESET

SHORT BOUTS OF MODERATE HIKING REDUCE STRESS HORMONES AND BOOST ENDORPHINS—EVEN WHEN YOU'RE SWEARING AT YOUR BOOTS.

Your nervous system counts effort, not elegance.

The REI Safety Spiral

I returned to REI for "supplies," by which I mean overpriced protein bars and an excuse to sniff dehydrated meals like a backcountry sommelier. Somewhere between the granola and the water filters, I asked the question I'd been quietly spiraling over:

"Do I need bear spray?"

The sales associate—Patagonia-clad, headlamp knowledge radiating off him—did not hesitate.

"Honestly, bear spray tends to piss bears off. Do not recommend."

"Okay, tha—"

"What you need to worry about is mountain lions. And you'll never hear them coming anyway."

"…"

"…"

So that was comforting. Excellent. I'll just add "stealth predator attack" to my to-do list.

I left with protein bars, a headlamp I didn't know how to use, and the creeping sense that the outdoors was basically a waiting room for my obituary.

Later, retelling it to a friend, I said, "Apparently, the safety plan is: stand tall, make noise, throw rocks, and don't run. So…menopause, but aimed toward stealthy giant cats with murder mitts."

Gear as Control

Looking back, I can see what I was really doing. I wasn't just buying stuff. I was buying the illusion of safety.

Boots wouldn't erase loneliness. A whistle wouldn't call back a marriage. A headlamp couldn't cut through the fog of guilt and shame I was carrying. But buying those things felt like forward motion, and forward motion counted.

The truth is, shopping felt like control. I could click *Buy Now* with confidence, even if it was back-ordered.

We are very good, culturally, at solving feelings with purchases—self-help stacks, meal kits, smartwatches that congratulate us for standing up. Outdoor culture adds its own spin: gear as identity. Buy the pack; become the person.

My pack got heavier not just with objects but with hopes: that the right items could carry me where courage hadn't yet.

And still—gear gave me stories. Rookie mistakes I could laugh at later, even if they weren't funny at the time. In a season when everything felt heavy, levity was worth the receipts.

The irony? The outdoors is clinically proven to calm the nervous system, but there I was trying to buy calm instead of walking toward it.

DECODER

GEAR ≠ CONFIDENCE
GEAR CAN'T GIVE YOU BELONGING.
IT CAN, HOWEVER, REMIND YOU TO SHOW UP.
CONFIDENCE STARTS IN MOTION, NOT IN CHECKOUT.

What I Carried

Here's what I eventually learned: Gear won't give you confidence. But sometimes carrying the thing—even if you never use it—helps you feel braver.

Gear can be a crutch. And sometimes a crutch is exactly what you need to start moving.

Gear can become a mirror. My pack was heavy because I was still trying to carry everything—safety, competence, image.

Women in midlife are experts at carrying: groceries, calendars, invisible labor, family expectations, the group chat. Gear was just the physical version of what I'd been hauling for decades. What I actually needed wasn't bear spray; I needed permission—to show up unprepared, awkward, and still worthy of being there.

REFLECT & RESET

WHAT ARE YOU STILL CARRYING?
LOOK THROUGH YOUR "GEAR"—THE LITERAL AND THE EMOTIONAL.
WHAT'S SAFETY, AND WHAT'S HABIT?
WHAT COULD YOU SET DOWN AND STILL FEEL SAFE ENOUGH TO MOVE?

Moving Forward

I thought gear would solve everything. That if I bought the right boots, the right pack, the right spray, I'd finally belong out there.

What gear gave me was blisters. It gave me paranoia about stealthy mountain lions. It gave me receipts for things I didn't know how to use.

It also gave me movement. A reason to step outside. A handful of stories to laugh at later. And that laughter turned out to be its own kind of safety.

You can't buy your way into confidence. You stumble into it.

And I stumbled plenty.

These days, the entryway tells the story better than I can: scuffed boots by the door, trekking poles leaning like tired sentries, a headlamp tossed in a catch-all bowl, half-eaten trail mix in the side pocket of a pack that finally fits. It makes me laugh now—the museum of "first tries."

Because even with all the gear in the world, there was no way around the next truth: some of my first steps would still be missteps.

But somewhere between those early attempts and now, something shifted. I stopped seeing myself as someone trying to belong outside and started seeing myself as someone who simply goes. Not perfectly. Not gracefully. But willingly.

If you've ever thought buying the right thing would finally make you ready, you already know this story.

You don't just walk out the door—you trip over a pile of first tries, lace up again, and keep going.

FIELD NOTES

REAL-WORLD GEAR GUIDE
Not sure what to buy, borrow, or skip?
My realistic starter list—plus the "cheap boots I regret" confessional—lives at RookieOutdoorWoman.com/trailanderror.
Updated each season, minus the hype and the stealth predators.

CHAPTER 8

False Starts

My first hikes as a newly single woman should have been simple. Fresh air. A short trail. A few hours to clear my head. Instead, they felt like auditions for a role I hadn't prepared for.

I wanted hiking to be cinematic: mist lifting off a lake, loons calling, me arriving at a vista with a dramatic sigh and great hair. Background music swells, credits roll, new life unlocked.

Yeah, no. Reality was sweat pooling in my sports bra, gnats forming a cult around my face, me squinting at a trail junction that looked like four identical options labeled *Good Luck.* The only soundtrack was my shoes chewing gravel and my internal monologue bargaining with my calves.

The air was thick enough to drink, the kind that makes you aware of every inch of skin. I told myself this was "healing," even as sunscreen dripped into my eyes.

Labels Lie

When I scouted trails online, I obsessed over those little difficulty ratings—easy, moderate, hard—as if they were gospel. They are not.

Sites try to be helpful ("ratings are assigned based on several factors"), but they're not standardized, your fitness varies by the day, and conditions change hour to hour. Treat them as vibes, not verdicts.

One "easy" loop turned out to be an uphill treadmill in disguise. The heat slapped me the moment I stepped out of the car. Ten minutes in, my shirt was glued to my back, and the incline was a polite but relentless "and up we go." I negotiated with my quads like they were hostile witnesses. At one point, I actually said, out loud, "You have got to be kidding me," to a slope that did not care.

Later I learned that what we call *easy* has nothing to do with terrain—it's about what our nervous system can handle that day. Stress and fatigue change your body's chemistry; the same hill can feel twice as steep when your brain's already carrying weight.

Then, two days later, I tried a "moderate" trail that felt like a neighborhood stroll—wide, shaded, barely a blip on my watch. I could've done it in flip-flops (I did not; see Chapter 7 and the Blister Debacle).

Conclusion: ratings can be useful, but they don't know your legs, your weather, or your day. And sometimes they're just wrong. Hence, Trail Ratings Are Lies.

TRAIL TRUTH

"EASY" IS A MOVING TARGET
YOUR BODY DECIDES THE RATING, NOT THE APP.
ENERGY, STRESS, SLEEP, HYDRATION—THOSE CHANGE THE
CLIMB MORE THAN ANY MILEAGE NUMBER EVER WILL.

The Heat, the Hills, the Humbling

Setup. July in eastern North Carolina—the kind of humid that makes the air feel like soup. I packed with optimism: cold water, a banana, two granola bars (aspirational), and my best *this is going to be great for your mental health* attitude. The listing called it *family-friendly*. How wholesome.

Conflict. Five minutes in, the bugs RSVP'd yes. Ten minutes in, my shoes pinched a spot I didn't know existed. I passed a couple in their seventies who breezed by chatting about tomatoes, while I huffed like a malfunctioning accordion. The sun hammered the exposed section, and I mentally drafted an apology to my future self for this plan.

Resolution. Halfway, I sat on a log. Sweat slid down my spine. A dragonfly hovered like an unhelpful coach. And the truth arrived: I wasn't just tired from the trail. I was tired from *all* of it—the paperwork, the parenting, the rebuilding. I had come looking for clarity. I got mosquitoes, mud, and the reminder that even "easy" things can feel impossible when you're holding everything else.

Still, the act of stopping—of admitting *this is enough for today*—quietly flipped a switch. That's recovery science 101: nervous-system down-regulation through rest. My brain didn't need more effort; it needed permission to pause.

DECODER

EFFORT ≠ FAILURE
SHOWING UP TIRED STILL COUNTS.
THE BODY LEARNS THROUGH MOTION, NOT PERFECTION.

The Quits

There were hikes I turned back on. No dramatic music, no failure montage. Just quiet decisions.

Quit #1 (Trail). A narrow path after heavy rain—slick, rooty, and tilted toward a creek that looked eager to adopt me. I stood there, weighing risk versus pride, and turned around. On the drive home, windows down, I felt equal parts disappointed and relieved. A month later, I went back on a dry day and finished it. Same trail, different conditions, different me.

Quit #2 (Not a trail). A post-divorce BBQ with too many people and too many questions asked too brightly. I smiled, made a plate, and lasted thirty-four minutes before telling myself the truth: I was done. I left early, sat in my car, and breathed. I used to count that as a failure. Now I call it listening.

Gen X translation: quitting used to mean weakness; turns out it's just emotional triage.

Even turning back means you started. Even cutting it short means you laced your shoes and tried. In those months, trying was not small.

Hiking helped me find my footing again; kayaking would test whether I could stay afloat. Literally and otherwise.

REFLECT & RESET

QUITTING AS BOUNDARY-SETTING
THINK OF ONE "QUIT" THAT WAS ACTUALLY PROTECTION.
WHAT DID STOPPING EARLY SPARE YOU FROM—INJURY, BURNOUT, PRETENDING?
NOT ALL EXITS ARE FAILURES; SOME ARE DETOURS THAT SAVE YOU FOR LATER.

How (Not) to Buy a Kayak

I had a perfectly good kayak. Sturdy. Reliable. Nothing wrong with it—except that it wasn't the lighter, sleeker one I'd been quietly eyeing for months. Something more agile. Maybe even something I could fish from without feeling like I was piloting a refrigerator.

Then one day, there it was: on sale. The temptation was instant. Cue the obsessive inner monologue: Should I? Shouldn't I?

The cost wasn't the issue. The problem was logistics. Specifically, I was alone. I no longer had the SUV that made kayak-hauling relatively painless. My current ride was a hatchback, and rooftop transport was the only option.

I'd actually stopped kayaking for a while because loading a boat on my roof felt like too much trouble. But I'm the one who preaches "get outside" like it's gospel. Time to practice what I post.

Step One: Acquire Kayak
With tie-downs in hand and confidence in short supply, I headed to the sporting goods store.

The first red flag? The staff had no idea how to get the kayak down from the top rack. Mild chaos followed. Possibly a small kayak avalanche. Eventually, I marched out, new boat on my shoulder, ready to conquer the roof rack and my life choices.

Step Two: Load Kayak Like a Grown-Ass Woman
Getting it onto the car required a maneuver best described as an awkward overhead press combined with mild cursing.

Because I live in the South, three separate men appeared out of nowhere to offer help.
Because I'm a Gen X woman raised on latchkey independence and stubborn pride, I politely declined every one of them.

I was going to do this. By. My. Damn. Self.

As I reasoned—while declining the third offer—if I was going to kayak alone, I needed to load alone, too. So, onward.

Step Three: The Tie-Down Tango
If you've never secured a kayak to a car roof, just know it involves:

- Ratchet straps (which are their own special brand of evil)
- Front and rear tie-downs (to prevent high-speed airborne incidents)
- Standing halfway inside your car to reach anything

It was awkward, but I was doing it. No meltdowns. No broken roof rack. I felt like a badass.

Then the sky darkened.

It began to sprinkle. By the time I reached the front strap, it was a full-on Southern gully washer—the kind that makes people pull over and pray.

I told myself it was a short drive and my halfway-done tie-downs were "probably fine."
(Narrator: They were absolutely not fine.)

Step Four: Cattywampus Chaos
One minute from the parking lot, the rear strap flapped loose. With no front tie-down tension, the kayak began drifting sideways like it had other plans.

The loose trap started singing the song of its people: flaaap-flaaap-flaaaap. I pulled onto a side street, tried to fix it, got drenched, and realized the kayak was now filling with rainwater. Because roof transport requires the kayak to ride upright, I had essentially created a portable bathtub strapped to my car.

Step Five: Limp Home and Regroup
I was a mile from home. Surely I could make it.

Ten white-knuckled minutes later—half certain the kayak would launch itself like a missile—I pulled into my garage. Soaked. Exhausted. Vaguely victorious.

Was it pretty? No.

Was it a mess? Absolutely.

Did I get that sucker home? Hell yes, I did.

Step Six: Accept Help (Eventually)
Once home, I tried to lift the kayak. No go. It was full of water and heavier than my pride.

I waited until my teenage sons—both six feet tall and unimpressed—got home. They helped me drain it, lift it down, and restore my dignity.

The moral? I got it done. I figured it out. And I learned what not to do next time.

Yes, I was too stubborn to accept help.

No, I won't always be.

But damn if I didn't feel proud—and maybe a little ridiculous.

FIELD-TESTED FAVORITE

THE FREEWAY KAZOO FIX
USE TWIST-AND-TUCK TAILS OR VELCRO STRAPS TO SILENCE THAT HIGH-SPEED STRAP SYMPHONY.
YOUR SANITY (AND HIGHWAY NEIGHBORS) WILL THANK YOU.

By the time I peeled off my wet clothes and dumped half a river out of that kayak, I realized something: every rookie story starts like this—equal parts chaos and determination. I wasn't chasing mastery. I was building muscle memory for persistence. Turns out "figuring it out" counts as progress, even when it looks like slapstick.

Progress in Disguise

False starts, I realized, are progress in disguise. They taught me to listen to my body, respect limits, and stop expecting the outdoors to hand me healing on a platter. Conditions shift. Labels lie. You figure it out as you go.

Psychologists call this error-based learning—the same principle that rewires your brain when you practice anything new. Every wrong turn lays down a map for the next attempt.

And it's not just me. Day hikers are consistently the largest share of National Park search-and-rescue cases (thousands a year) because lots of us underestimate distance, heat, terrain, or our own bandwidth. One NPS snapshot found roughly 43 percent of SARs involve day hikers; the pattern repeats across parks. Translation: "This should be easy" gets a lot of people in trouble.

So if your "easy" turns into "nope," you're in crowded company.

OUTDOOR EFFECT

FAILURE AS FAST LEARNING
YOUR BRAIN CEMENTS MEMORY UP TO 70 PERCENT BETTER AFTER AN INITIAL FAILURE THAN AFTER EFFORTLESS SUCCESS.
EACH MISTAKE IS A NEUROLOGICAL BOOKMARK: TRY AGAIN, BUT SMARTER.

Every Step Still Counts

Here's the truth I finally landed on: false starts are still starts. They're proof of motion. Of courage. Of trying.

Every "failed" hike, every turned-around paddle, every retreat to the car was still movement. Each one whispered: "You're not stuck."

False starts weren't the end of the story—they were the messy middle. Middle chapters are where stamina grows, not sparkle. The outdoors taught me that healing isn't cinematic; it's repetitive.

And even in the middle, I wasn't alone. That's where the story turns next: the friends who started showing up in ways boots and gear never could.

If a blaze marks the path you missed, friends are the next blaze you finally see—bright, steady, saying *this way*—when you lift your eyes.

FIELD NOTES

TRAIL RATINGS ARE LIES
Curious why "easy" so often isn't?
The full essay and updated rating decoder live at
RookieOutdoorWoman.com/trailanderror.
Spoiler: humidity and midlife knees aren't in the algorithm.

CHAPTER 9

The Friends Who Showed Up

People love to say you find out who your true friends are during a divorce. I used to roll my eyes at that–another tidy cliché people reach for when real words fail them. But it turned out to be true in a way I didn't expect.

I did lose people. Couples we used to see on Saturday nights who chose a side that wasn't mine. Group texts that went suspiciously quiet. The awkward silences I'd expected showed up on schedule.

But here's what I didn't expect: the steady, undramatic presence that stitched me back together–coffee by coffee, text by text, laugh by laugh. Not rescues. Not grand gestures. Just ordinary faithfulness when I was coming apart at the seams.

There's a name for it in the research: co-regulation. Someone else's calm helps your nervous system downshift when yours is fried. I didn't have the term then; I just knew I breathed easier next to them.

The Shape of Presence

On paper, my divorce was amicable. We were civil, committed to parenting together, determined not to torch the whole thing on our way out. From the outside, that looked like a win.

Inside, it was still brutal. The grief. The guilt. The shame. The logistics that never ended. Even when you agree to part, unraveling a marriage yanks out roots you thought were permanent.

My friends couldn't fix that. They didn't try. They showed up.

The kitchen table. A friend sat across from me while condensation slid down our iced coffees, the ring of water slowly blooming on the wood. We didn't rush. She asked, "Where does it hurt most today?" and then let silence do its job. Every so often, she'd nod, push the napkin pile toward me, or say, "You're not crazy. This is hard." It was a master class in not solving.

That silence felt like shade on a scorching day—protective, not empty.

The nightly texts. Around 10:42 p.m., my phone would light up: a meme, a three-line check-in, a photo of her dog in pajamas. Sometimes I couldn't reply. Sometimes I sent back a single heart. Either way, it landed like a blanket: someone is with you, even when you're alone in the house.

Tiny pings, measurable effect. Loneliness spikes stress chemistry; even small signals of connection can lower the volume.

REFLECT & RESET

WHO STEADIES YOUR NERVOUS SYSTEM?
NAME THE PERSON WHOSE CALM SLOWS YOUR PULSE.
SEND THEM A ONE-LINE THANK-YOU.
PRESENCE HEALS FASTER THAN PEP TALKS.

Sunday pool invites. In the summer, a group adopted me for Sunday afternoons. I'd swing by custody pick-up later that night in a suit and cover-up. No one asked for updates. We gossiped about work, traded sunscreen, and argued about whether prosecco counts as electrolytes. It was unremarkable and exactly what I needed.

That kind of easy ritual is medicine. Routine tells the body: you're safe enough to exhale.

None of them offered solutions. They offered presence. And that was exactly the medicine I could absorb.

Later, I realized what made those moments powerful: none of them tried to fix me. They held space instead of solutions.

TRAIL TRUTH

PRESENCE > PEP TALKS
YOU DON'T NEED THE PERFECT WORDS.
YOU JUST NEED TO STAY.

DECODER

PRESENCE ≠ FIXING
YOU CAN'T REPAIR SOMEONE'S STORM.
YOU CAN HOLD THE UMBRELLA UNTIL IT PASSES.

The TED Talk

That presence didn't always arrive as a chair pulled out or groceries on the porch; sometimes it came in the form of a new way to think. One friend gave me something more: a reframe.

Early on, when I was stumbling over the words *we're separating*, she sent me a TED Talk.[1] The speaker argued that divorce isn't fail-

---

[1] TEDx Talks. "Real Talk about Divorce | Christian Family | TEDxColumbus." YouTube Video. *YouTube*, January 9, 2020. https://www.youtube.com/watch?v=_7S6FTdl4A0.

ure—it's evolution. A turning point when two people stop growing together and move apart.

That idea cracked something open. I had been carrying the cultural script that divorce equals broken. For the first time, I felt something loosen inside me, like maybe I wasn't defective for wanting out. The reframe didn't erase grief or dissolve guilt, but it softened the shame. It let me consider that I wasn't quitting; I was changing.

Language matters. Rename a thing and your body often follows— shoulders drop, jaw unclenches, breath returns.

It echoed what the trail was already teaching me: just as "easy" hikes can wreck you, "successful" marriages can still end. Labels lie. Progress sometimes looks like turning around, picking a new line, or admitting the map you were using no longer fits the terrain.

Now, when people learned of my divorce and said they were sorry, I said, *No, you can say congratulations.*

For those of us raised to walk it off, congratulations felt rebellious— permission to celebrate survival instead of apologizing for it.

OUTDOOR EFFECT

MINDSET = CHEMISTRY
REFRAMING STRESS AS "CHALLENGE" INSTEAD OF "THREAT" MEASURABLY REDUCES CORTISOL AND HEART-RATE SPIKES.
SOMETIMES THE TRAIL YOU RENAME IS INSIDE YOUR OWN HEAD.

Presence, Not Performance

Later, online, I joked about blisters and bear spray, about bailing on a hike halfway and calling it a win because no one is watching, about tent sleep being a scam. Those posts landed because they were funny—but also because they were honest.

Women are trained to perform okay-ness. Smile for the kids. Keep the calendar spinning. Hold the house and everyone in it.

The most radical thing my friends did was refuse that script on my behalf. They didn't ask me to be inspirational. They let me be messy, bored, tired, and undone. They brought crackers and seltzer and sat through the ugly-cry. They didn't keep score.

It turns out honesty is contagious; their unflinching made it easier for me to tell the truth without dressing it up.

That permission—to be witnessed without performing—was the oxygen I didn't know I was missing.

Trail Markers

They were my blazes.

On a hike, you don't always notice the paint on trees until you're not sure you're still on the trail. Then you look up, and the small rectangle of color is pure relief.

I think about the day I wandered off a loop and felt panic humming in my teeth. I stopped, made myself breathe, scanned the trees, and there it was: a blaze I'd walked past in my hurry. *Okay. This way.*

Friends did that for me. A text. A chair pulled out. A "come over, we're making tacos." Little flashes of guidance that said: you're not lost; keep going.

Social scientists would call it *belonging cues*. I called it not drowning.

And the way they showed me the trail wasn't dramatic—it was ordinary, steady, human.

TRAIL TRUTH

LOOK UP
THE BLAZE IS USUALLY CLOSER THAN YOU THINK.
KEEP SCANNING. HELP IS OFTEN ALREADY WAVING.

Nobody swooped in with a five-point plan for reinvention. They showed up with groceries when my brain couldn't plan dinner. They said, "Target run?" and let me wander the aisles like a civilian. They looped my arm through theirs on a walk and didn't ask for an update every ten feet. They made a place for me on couches, at picnic tables, and in bleachers.

It wasn't spectacular. It was steady. And steady is what rebuilds you.

Bodies heal in steady states—sleep, routine, sunlight, small laughter. Friendship gave me all four without a prescription.

OUTDOOR EFFECT

FRIENDSHIP = INFRASTRUCTURE
REGULAR SOCIAL CONTACT LOWERS PERCEIVED STRESS AND IMPROVES SLEEP.
YOUR FRIENDS ARE PART OF YOUR NERVOUS SYSTEM ARCHITECTURE—KEEP THEM MAINTAINED.

Because in the messy middle of a divorce, you don't need a rescue. You need reminders: *You matter. You're loved. You're not as alone as your living room feels at 11 p.m.*

The Ground Beneath My Feet

Looking back, I can see those friendships were the ground beneath my feet. They didn't shorten the climb or flatten the trail. They kept me upright long enough to take the next step.

In midlife, when old structures shift–marriage, routines, who's our couple friends–friendships become infrastructure. They're the bridges you cross when familiar roads are closed.

And like real bridges, the magic is mostly in the engineering you don't see–group chats, calendars, soup dropped on porches.

With their steadiness, I began to imagine something new waiting for me. Not a destination yet. Not even a clear direction. Just a name, a whisper, an identity sitting quietly until I was ready to claim it.

It would surface first on the trail, then on the page.

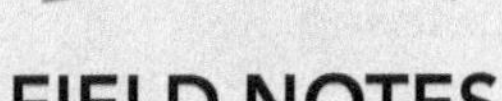

FIELD NOTES

ROOKIE FRIENDSHIP PACK
FOR THE RESEARCH ON CO-REGULATION, MIDLIFE FRIENDSHIP, AND THE "BELONGING CUES" THAT INSPIRED THIS CHAPTER, VISIT ROOKIEOUTDOORWOMAN.COM/TRAILANDERROR.
INCLUDES MY RECOMMENDED READS AND A PRINTABLE *CONNECTION MAP* FOR YOUR OWN TRAIL NETWORK.

Part 2 Conclusion: Tripped on the Trailhead

Looking back, I can see how clumsy those first steps were.

I craved space but didn't know what to do with it. I bought gear that gave me blisters and paranoia instead of confidence. I trusted labels that lied to me and trails that humbled me. I camped for less than a night before bolting home with my dignity stuffed in the trunk.

None of it looked like progress. It looked like a blooper reel.

But here's the thing: every stumble was still movement. Every blister, every wrong turn, every "nope" on a so-called easy hike was proof that I wasn't stuck. And when I couldn't stand steady on my own, my friends were there—trail markers reminding me I wasn't lost, even when I felt like I was.

That was the quiet magic of this season: I didn't have to be good at the outdoors to start belonging in it. I didn't have to be brave to keep moving. I just had to show up—awkward, unprepared, sometimes a little ridiculous—and trust that was enough.

Those early trips, those rookie mistakes, those late-night texts and coffee shop lifelines—they didn't make me an expert. They made me a beginner who kept trying.

And somewhere in the middle of the blisters and the laughter and the quiet presence of women who refused to let me disappear, a new name started whispering in the background. A name I wasn't ready to claim yet. But it was there, waiting.

That's where the story turns next.

PART 3
MUDDY BUT MOVING

By the time I claimed the name *Rookie Outdoor Woman*, I still wasn't sure what I was doing. But I knew this much: I wasn't standing still anymore.

The craving for space had pulled me outside. The gear fiascos and false starts taught me that blisters and bad advice don't mean you quit. And the friends who showed up steadied me long enough to keep going.

Now it was time to move. Not gracefully. Not strategically. Just—forward.

Forward looked like tents collapsing at 3 a.m., sliding sideways in a kayak I could barely get on top of the car, and fishing trips where the only thing I caught was a sunburn and a story. It wasn't the glossy-magazine version of adventure—no fairy lights, no sunrise abs. My outdoors were mud, bug spray, and the occasional raccoon fight club outside the tent. And somehow, inside the chaos, I started to find myself.

This part of the story isn't about getting it right. It's about saying yes anyway—finding lessons in the mess, laughter in the failures, and a new identity forming step by shaky step.

Because momentum doesn't require grace. It just requires movement.

The Name That Sat There

I had a name before I had a story: *Rookie Outdoor Woman.*

I claimed the Substack handle one evening in a fit of optimism, convinced I had something to say to other midlife women craving the outdoors. And then… I did nothing. The page sat blank for over a year, collecting digital dust while I tried to figure out whether I even belonged out there.

It turns out even digital doors can be hard to walk through when you're still learning how to leave your own house without apologizing for it.

The Origin Scene

It was late—house quiet, kids asleep, dishwasher clicking through its tired rhythms. I sat at the kitchen island with my laptop open, a glass of red half-finished, the overhead light turning the screen into a small stage. I typed the name, stared, backspaced, retyped.

This sounds ridiculous, I thought. *You? Outdoors?*

Then another voice: *No. This is mine.*

The word rookie made me smile. It didn't pretend I knew what I was doing. It didn't demand a summit selfie or a lifetime of trail cred. It offered truth in lowercase letters. I hit "create," and the handle snapped into place like a puzzle piece I'd been hunting for under the couch.

And then the page just…sat there, waiting.

Naming is the tug on the thread. What comes next is the slow, awkward unravel that makes room for something new.

TRAIL TRUTH

A NAME IS A TRAILHEAD
CLAIMING THE NAME IS THE FIRST STEP.
THE HIKE IS EVERYTHING THAT HAPPENS
AFTER YOU STEP THROUGH.

The Blank Page

That empty Substack space mocked me. Who was I to write about hiking when I couldn't even pick the right shoes? Who was I to claim an outdoors identity when my version of adventure was bailing halfway through "easy" trails and calling it a win if I didn't cry on the drive home?

Writing felt impossible. Claiming a voice felt arrogant. I filled my days with parenting, work, and logistics—the endless churn of keeping a life from collapsing. The name *Rookie Outdoor Woman* waited patiently. I did not.

The blank page became a mirror for everything else: divorce had handed me a new, unmarked chapter of my life and said, "Write." And blank-page energy is terrifying. At least a blister gives feedback. A blank page just stares back, daring you to go first.

Here's the truth: claiming an identity before you feel ready is awkward—like putting on clothes a size too big, too bold, too obvious. But sometimes naming is the first step toward becoming. Rookie Outdoor Woman didn't ask me to fake expertise. It gave me permission to be a beginner on purpose.

Midlife women are told to "reinvent" with polish–second acts, glow-ups, strategic pivots. We're rarely given permission to start at zero. Kids get endless grace to learn. Adults get performance reviews.

The name let me opt out of performance and into practice.

Gen X edition: we were raised to "figure it out and don't make it weird." Fine. I figured it out in public, tried not to make it weird, and aimed for honest instead of impressive. Once I stopped trying so hard, the quiet got louder.

REFLECT & RESET

NAME THE BLANK PAGE
WHAT EMPTY SQUARE IS STARING AT YOU RIGHT NOW?
WRITE ITS NAME DOWN. DON'T FIX IT YET–JUST NAME IT.

Something Wild, Waiting

And yet, the name lingered like a whisper I couldn't ignore. I kept hearing the cadence of what I wanted to say:

Hey there, nature-curious. If you've ever looked at the outdoors and thought, "I'd like nature, but make it low effort," you're in the right place. Women 40+ who want practical tips, real talk, and a little sarcasm. Start hiking, camping, kayaking–or just sit on a rock in peace.

When I finally wrote the launch post–*Something Wild This Way Comes*–I admitted what I'd been circling all along: "Outdoorsy" didn't have to mean elite or extreme. It could mean messy, midlife, figuring it out as you go.

But before I could say that out loud, I had to sit with the silence. The long pause. The not-knowing.

Silence isn't the absence of courage; sometimes it's the staging area. Curiosity builds the scaffolding while fear fills out the permit forms.

Claiming the name turned out to be scarier than claiming the outdoors. Tents don't judge you. Publishing does. Still, the first time someone wrote back "same," the room tilted. The page wasn't a mirror anymore; it was a window.

FIELD NOTES

LAUNCH ESSAY – "SOMETHING WILD THIS WAY COMES"
READ THE FIRST ROOKIE OUTDOOR WOMAN POST THAT STARTED IT ALL AT ROOKIEOUTDOORWOMAN.COM/TRAILANDERROR.
PROOF THAT HESITATION STILL COUNTS AS MOVEMENT.

TRAIL TRUTH

PRACTICE > PERFORMANCE
WHEN YOU'RE BUILDING A LIFE, NOT A RÉSUMÉ,
REPS MATTER MORE THAN POLISH.

The Year of Almost

For a year, I almost wrote. Almost hiked consistently. Almost said yes to opportunities. Almost stepped into a bigger version of myself.

Almost looks like:

- Itinerary tabs open for a weekend cabin…that I never booked.
- Drafts titled "Start Here" and "Your First Hike" that stalled at paragraph two.
- A cart full of boot socks and a trail-map app…left to expire.
- A park program on my calendar…replaced by laundry and "I'll go next week."

Almost isn't glamorous. It doesn't make a good caption. But almost is movement. It's walking circles around the trailhead while your courage catches up. It's practice in disguise.

Behavior scientists call it *shaping*—tiny approximations of the thing you're trying to do until your brain stops panicking. My approximations looked like parking at a trailhead and answering emails with the windows down. Not heroic. Helpful.
Eventually, almost stopped being enough.

FIELD-TESTED FAVORITE

THE 5-MINUTE RULE

IF IT FEELS IMPOSSIBLE, PROMISE YOURSELF FIVE MINUTES. YOU CAN LEAVE AFTER THAT. YOU RARELY WILL. READ MORE ABOUT THE 5-MINUTE RULE IN ACTION AT ROOKIEOUTDOORWOMAN.COM/TRAILANDERROR.

Micro-Yeses (How the Page Finally Opened)

The handle existed. The fear existed. What I didn't have were micro-yeses—ridiculously small commitments that let me move without drama.

I made a list on a sticky note titled **No Heroics.** It lived on my laptop.

- Yes to "draft ugly." I opened a new doc and wrote three bad paragraphs about blister tape. They were awful. They were progress.
- Yes to "publish tiny." I hit post on a 300-word note about feeling stupid in an aisle of water filters. People wrote back with their own "stupid" aisles.
- Yes to "showing my work." I screenshot a map, circled the wrong turn I took, and called it science.
- Yes to "office hours at the park." I took calls from a picnic table and typed with sunscreen on my hands.

The dopamine wasn't fireworks; it was a trickle. But trickles fill canteens.

REFLECT & RESET

ONE MICRO-YES
WHAT'S ONE 5 PERCENT MOVE THAT WOULD MAKE YOUR IDENTITY-IN-WAITING MORE REAL THIS WEEK?
WRITE IT. SCHEDULE IT. KEEP IT TINY ON PURPOSE.

Belonging, Lightly

Belonging arrived quietly, not as a crowd's applause, but as a single voice saying, *I went too.*

For months, isolation had felt heavy and airless, like carrying a backpack full of rocks I couldn't set down. This was lighter–belonging as a soft nudge, not a spotlight. A reminder that I wasn't wandering alone, even if I still felt like a beginner.

The outdoors had been teaching me that lesson all along: you don't need the hardest trail to feel alive; you just need a place to stand, air in your lungs, and permission to notice what helps. The page became that place too.

Attention Restoration Theory would call it *soft fascination.* I called it *not spiraling for fifteen minutes while I wrote about shade.*

And then came the moment that shifted everything.

I hovered over the "publish" button, heart racing. I wasn't ready. I was just tired of waiting.

Click.

For a second, nothing happened—then the post bloomed on the screen, the way a view appears when you round the last bend. Panic flared. I slammed the laptop shut as if I'd just let a bird loose in the kitchen. Then I opened it again and reread my own words: *you don't have to summit before sunrise to belong out here.*

That first post wasn't a declaration. It was a dare, a test to see if I could say out loud what I already knew inside: I am here—still messy, still rookie—and that is enough.

The name had been sitting there for a year, patient as a trailhead sign, waiting for me to step onto the path.

Next up: the small yeses that kept me moving—community, routine, and a backpack that finally fit.

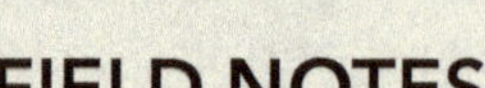

FIELD NOTES

Start Here Guide
New to the Rookie Outdoor Woman trail?
Find beginner resources, community links, and every "rookie win" story at RookieOutdoorWoman.com/trailanderror.

CHAPTER 11

Every Trail Has a Story (So Does Every Scar)

Transformation didn't start with a leap.

It started with a whisper of *yes*.

Not the cinematic kind. Not *sign up for Everest* or *quit your job and move to Bali*. My old image of change was always glossy—grand gestures, perfect lighting, a soundtrack that swells on cue.

Real life was quieter. It looked like saying yes to a 1.5-mile loop on a Tuesday. Yes to a weekend in a tiny cabin with too many snacks. Yes to a weird opportunity that made my stomach flip. Stack enough small yeses, and the ground shifts anyway.

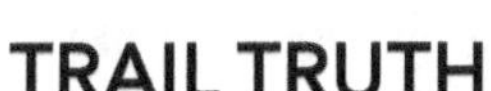

TRAIL TRUTH

BIG CHANGE STARTS IN WHISPERS
THE MONTAGE COMES LATER.
REAL TRANSFORMATION STARTS WITH
A QUIET *SURE, WHY NOT.*

The Hike That Turned Into Wine

I bailed on a hike halfway through.

Everything hurt. My feet filed formal complaints. My hamstrings staged a walkout. The trail was dusty, the flies were unionized, and the "high point" had zero view—just trees hoarding all the scenery.

At the junction, I said it out loud: "Nope." A squirrel judged me. I ignored him.

I turned around, limped to the car, and drove straight to a winery where I walked in sweaty, trail-dirty, and looking like a woman who had fought a shrub and lost. Fun fact: They were setting up for a wedding later that evening, so I looked supremely out of place.

"Seat for one?" the host asked, politely making a point of not staring at the leaf in my hair.

"For one," I said, "and a rosé that forgives."

Cold glass. Gorgeous breeze on the patio. A view of the mountain I ghosted. Cheese board that did not require altitude. My notebook and pen waiting.

It didn't feel like progress. It felt like quitting. Later I realized it was its own kind of yes: yes to listening to my body, yes to changing the plan, yes to joy even when it didn't look like a summit photo.

The body keeps scorecards we can't always read. When I stopped fighting the hill, my pulse slowed, my breath steadied, and the wine probably did less for me than the parasympathetic reset of finally sitting down.

That winery "yes" was quiet, almost private. The next one was anything but.

OUTDOOR EFFECT

REST IS A SKILL

STOPPING MID-TRAIL ACTIVATES THE PARASYMPATHETIC "REST-AND-DIGEST" SYSTEM.

SOMETIMES RECOVERY *IS* THE WORKOUT.

DECODER

REST ≠ QUITTING

PAUSING IS HOW THE STORY CATCHES ITS BREATH.

YOU'RE NOT FALLING BEHIND—YOU'RE ABSORBING THE VIEW.

The Skydiving Yes

Then there were the bigger yeses.

When the commander mentioned a chance to jump with the Golden Knights, I said yes before the sensible parts of my brain convened a meeting.

Fast-forward: harness snug, goggles on, the plane door yawning open to bright sky and loud wind.

The rush sounded like the inside of a jet engine. The air slapped my cheeks into a smile I couldn't stop. For a heartbeat, my stomach argued with gravity; then we were falling, and the fear flipped into awe. I watched the patchwork ground tilt toward me and thought, *I am still here. Still willing. Still alive enough to fling myself into new air.*

That yes didn't mend everything, but it echoed on the ground: if I could say yes at 120 mph, I could say yes to a lot of smaller, quieter things with my feet on dirt.

OUTDOOR EFFECT

THE AWE RESET
MOMENTS OF AWE—SKY-HIGH OR TRAIL-SIDE—QUIET STRESS PATH-WAYS AND SPARK MEANING-MAKING.
FEAR TURNS INTO PERSPECTIVE AT FREE-FALL SPEED.

The Quiet Yeses

The magic wasn't one yes. It was the stack.

- Yes to walking when the couch made a persuasive case.
- Yes to a flat trail, even if my ego wanted "strenuous."
- Yes to packing the car, knowing the tent would leak, and I'd invent new swear words at 2 a.m.
- Yes to kayaking, even if the roof racks required a TED Talk and a neighbor named Stan.
- Yes to texting a friend, "Are you up?" and leaving her be if she wasn't.
- Yes to writing the first Substack post with my heart hammering like I'd released a bird in the kitchen.
- Yes to stopping when my calves said, "Absolutely not."
- Yes to starting again two days later.

Quick. Punchy. Small. That rhythm built a muscle memory: *I can do this. I can try.*

Somewhere in those small yeses, I said yes to letting someone in—slowly, carefully, the way you test a crossing after rain. And that was the quiet turn I didn't see coming.

Because the yeses didn't just move me outdoors. They moved me back into myself.

Every yes became a permission slip: to rest, to risk, to laugh, to fail. To be a rookie without apology.

We tell midlife women to be resilient, to reinvent, to bounce back with a tidy arc. What we don't say enough is that reinvention sneaks in on ordinary, unglamorous yeses. One afternoon walk. One RSVP. One call. One post.

You look up months later and realize you've built a whole new path out of decisions no one applauded at the time.

Gen X translation: we were taught to under-react. So the quiet yeses felt subversive—a rebellion by calm.

REFLECT & RESET

THREE TINY YESES
LIST THREE YESES FROM THIS WEEK—MOVEMENT, REST, OR COURAGE ALL COUNT.
THEY'RE NOT SMALL; THEY'RE COMPOUND INTEREST.

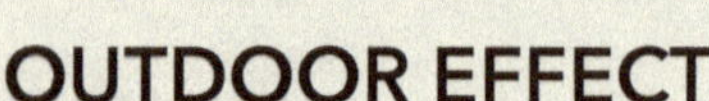

OUTDOOR EFFECT

MICRO-GOAL CHEMISTRY
EACH SMALL SUCCESS TRIGGERS A DOPAMINE HIT—PROOF YOUR BRAIN LOVES INCREMENTAL PROGRESS MORE THAN GRAND PLANS. PROGRESS FEELS GOOD BECAUSE IT'S BITE-SIZED.

Momentum, Messy and Real

When I look back, I don't remember the days I stayed careful. I remember the yeses. The messy, ungraceful, sometimes hilarious choices that moved me forward while I was still covered in mud.

The blisters? I said yes to better socks and another mile next week.

The failed hike? I said yes to a winery and a laugh.

The leap from the plane? I said yes to the ground rising to meet me—and to the life waiting when it did.

Momentum doesn't require grace. It requires movement.

And if every trail has a story, then every scar does too—proof that I showed up, that I learned something, that I kept saying yes. The scars became trail markers—small, imperfect, permanent reminders that healing isn't about erasing; it's about remembering how far you've walked.

Next: how those yeses became a map I could actually follow.

FIELD-TESTED FAVORITE

KEEP A TRAIL LOG OF YESES
NOTEBOOK, PHONE NOTE, OR WINE-STAINED NAPKIN—WRITE THEM DOWN.
PROOF YOU'RE ALREADY IN MOTION BEATS ANY PEP TALK.

FIELD NOTES

MICRO-YES MAP
DOWNLOAD THE PRINTABLE TRACKER FOR SMALL WINS AND VISIBLE MOMENTUM AT ROOKIEOUTDOORWOMAN.COM/TRAILANDERROR.
PROOF THAT REPETITION—NOT REINVENTION—BUILDS CHANGE.

CHAPTER 12

Mud on My Boots

Progress wasn't elegant. It was messy and real and enough.

It looked like me sliding on wet leaves, slapping at mosquitoes, and wondering—out loud—what exactly I had signed up for.

It was a late-spring loop after rain, the kind of green that hums. The trail was more suggestion than surface; slick clay clung to my soles until my boots weighed approximately one toddler each. I pinballed between saplings, arms out for balance, muttering negotiations with gravity. A gnat committed to a long-term relationship with my left eye.

When I finally stopped, panting, I noticed I'd smeared dirt across my cheek like a warrior who'd lost the instructions. Standing there, wet to the shins and very attractive in my swamp-chic, I realized: this is what progress looks like right now—muddy, bitten, unphotogenic, and real.

TRAIL TRUTH

GROWTH RARELY ARRIVES IN CLEAN CLOTHES
IF YOU'RE SPOTLESS, YOU PROBABLY HAVEN'T LEFT THE
TRAILHEAD YET.

Why I Should Not Be Left Unsupervised near Boats

Getting the kayak onto the water should have been simple. (We're skipping the roof-rack opera; that premiered in an earlier chapter.) This was just the launch: a sloped, algae-slick ramp, a crosswind with opinions, and me narrating to myself like a coach I didn't hire.

You lift weights, you can do this.

Slide…slide…no, not sideways…okay, sideways.

Three men hovered in polite formation–"Need a hand?"–and my Gen X independence snarled on cue. I paddled out backward, corrected with the grace of a confused crab, and forty minutes later paddled back into a downpour so epic my shoes made the kind of squelch that predicts athlete's foot.

Later came the duck-hunting boat, which also doubled as a fishing vessel: a flat-bottomed personality test with an engine powered mostly by hope. We eased into a shallow cove, tapped a submerged log, and spun in place like a malfunctioning Roomba. I swung over the side into thigh-deep water that went instantly up to my dignity, shoved us off the log, and whooped in relief.

Different crafts, same lesson: independence is admirable until it becomes a liability. The outdoors kept reminding me that sometimes help is the skill.

And of course, not every adventure was a solo act. Some required a whole cast, chaos included.

OUTDOOR EFFECT

TEAM CHEMISTRY
COOPERATIVE OUTDOOR TASKS—CARRYING GEAR, PADDLING TANDEM—DROP CORTISOL FASTER THAN SOLO EFFORT.
COMMUNITY IS ITS OWN REGULATION SYSTEM.

DECODER

HELP ≠ WEAKNESS
STRENGTH ISN'T DOING IT ALONE.
IT'S KNOWING WHEN TEAMWORK KEEPS YOU AFLOAT.

Tent Disasters (Family Edition)

Tent sleep is a scam. Instagram shows families glowing under fairy lights; reality is cots that judge you and air mattresses that give up at 2:17 a.m.

The rainy night. The forecast said "light showers." The sky said, "Watch this." Around midnight, the first drop tapped the fly like suspense music; ten minutes later, it was a drumline. Our rainfly was apparently one inch shorter than the storm's ambitions.
A cold line of water marched across someone's pillow, and we launched full family triage: towel levee, pot under the drip, me holding a flashlight while their dad crawled out to re-stake the fly like a NASCAR pit crew for tents. We woke up damp, cranky, and bonded by the smell of wet socks—and victory.

The raccoon circus. Different trip, same chaos. At 10 p.m., kid giggles. At eleven, whisper-shouting. At midnight, an outside thump and the rip-zip of a trash-bag audition. I unzipped the door to find a masked committee mid-heist. One raccoon made eye contact and continued rearranging our snack hierarchy. The boys thought it was the funniest thing they'd ever seen; I shooed with a spatula like a frazzled camp counselor while their dad re-tied the food bag.

We were bone-tired the next day and weirdly proud—only lightly mugged and full of stories. These were not solo feats. They were family misadventures—loud, imperfect, ours.

TRAIL TRUTH

SHARED MISERY = MEMORY GLUE
WHAT'S PAINFUL NOW WILL BE
HILARIOUS LATER—TAKE NOTES.

OUTDOOR EFFECT

AFTER-RAIN RESET
POST-STORM FOREST AIR CARRIES NEGATIVE IONS THAT CALM THE NERVOUS SYSTEM AND LIFT MOOD.
NATURE'S VERSION OF AN EXHALE.

The Mess as Teacher

None of these were highlight-reel moments. They were messy, chaotic, and often uncomfortable. But every slip, every soggy sock, every sleepless night taught me something:

- *In the moment:* Why am I doing this?
- *A week later:* That's where the growth happened.
- *Universally:* Midlife women already know this truth—progress is rarely graceful; it's persistent.

Discomfort isn't fatal. Imperfection is survivable. Laughter is equipment.

Neuroscientists call this error-based learning: your brain rewires fastest when you mess up and try again. Turns out my nervous system was running a long-term field study called *How to Be Okay in Chaos.*

The mud washed off. The bug bites healed. The raccoons moved on to terrorize a different campsite.

What stayed was the reminder that forward is still forward—even when it looks ridiculous.

By my door now: a lineup of boots wearing dried clay like badges, the kayak paddle leaning cockeyed in the corner, a coil of tie-down straps that no longer sing on the freeway. Evidence of chaos. Evidence of movement. A museum of tries.

When I walk past them, I don't see failure gear. I see data—proof that joy survived the mud, that humor beat frustration, that motion kept happening.

That's the hidden curriculum of midlife adventure: chaos doesn't cancel growth; it documents it. And every woman I've shared these stories with has nodded in recognition. We're all improvising—on trails, in marriages, in careers—and the relief comes from realizing the chaos is shared, not shameful.

REFLECT & RESET

FORWARD ANYWAY

THINK OF ONE MUDDY, AWKWARD, OR "FAILED" TRY THAT TAUGHT YOU SOMETHING REAL.

WHAT PROOF OF PROGRESS DID IT LEAVE BEHIND?

FIELD NOTES

ROOKIE OUTDOOR WOMAN GUIDE

EXPLORE REAL-WORLD FIXES AND FIELD-TESTED HACKS FROM THESE ADVENTURES AT ROOKIEOUTDOORWOMAN.COM/TRAILANDERROR. EVERYTHING THAT SURVIVED MUD, LEAKS, AND RACCOONS—SO YOU DON'T HAVE TO LEARN IT TWICE.

CHAPTER 13

Nature Doesn't Care About Your Deadlines

Not all lessons came from therapy or books. Some came from blisters, broken poles, and bathrooms I still have nightmares about.

Rookie misadventures, rapid-fire:

- Forgot bug spray; became a buffet with legs.
- Sunblock "mist" met crosswind; achieved abstract shoulder art in lobster red.
- Trekking-pole tip snapped off like a breadstick two miles from the car.
- Sleeping-bag zipper welded shut at 2:03 a.m.; emerged like a butterfly with regrets.
- Trail mix melted into a single, peanut-raisin geode.
- Took the "scenic detour" and invented a new loop called *Where the Hell Are We.*

None of that was glamorous. All of it taught me something.

Each mishap became a crash course in humility. Nature doesn't care about your inbox or your goals; it only cares that you hydrate, notice, and keep your balance when the trail turns slick. It was the first teacher I couldn't impress—no performance review, no extra credit, just consequences and quiet grace when I finally listened.

And just when I thought the lessons were confined to trails and mud, the water offered its own curriculum.

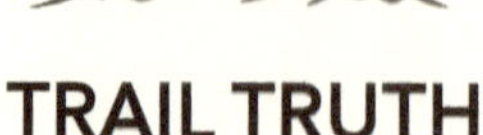

TRAIL TRUTH

READINESS IS OVERRATED
CURIOSITY IS ENOUGH.
THAT'S THE ONLY CREDENTIAL NATURE ASKS FOR.

The Bathroom Boat

We booked a make-up deep-sea charter–the fishing version of a blind date. Six spots on the boat, two of us, and four strangers who became characters before we even hit the Gulf Stream: a solo guy whose family chose sleep over seas, two old college buddies on a decades-late reunion, and an elderly widower who slept in the marina lot so he wouldn't miss the trip. Tell me that isn't a screenplay setup.

Before we talk fish, let's talk Dramamine and one tiny bathroom. We left at the butt-crack of dawn (apparently fish ignore banker's hours), and I pre-gamed seasickness with enough medication to feel like I'd been sedated by a Victorian doctor. Yes, I dozed off on the ride out. Also: eight humans, serious swells, one bathroom. I've seen crime scenes with less carnage. *CSI: Maritime Edition* could have taken samples. Gentlemen, aim is a skill.

Somewhere between nausea and horror, I realized the ocean was enforcing its own version of mindfulness. My brain could spin only so long before the horizon demanded attention. The waves forced rhythm; I either fought or floated. Eventually, I floated.

Stress science–basically the study of how our bodies downshift once the threat response exhausts itself–calls that recalibration: your body dropping into sync with motion once resistance burns out. I just called it survival.

Then we hit the Gulf Stream, and everything turned glorious. Sun high, salt spray in my face, adrenaline finally beating the meds. We took turns in the "big chair," strapped in and grinning; the tally included blackfin tuna, mahi, and a show-off wahoo. We cheered, filmed, and helped our widower re-live a day he'll be sending to his grandkids.

On the ride back, one guy dozed and did a full bench somersault when a wave hit. He was fine. I laughed first, asked questions later. (Not proud. A little proud.)

Bonus: our slip was a few down from *Fishing Frenzy* of *Wicked Tuna* fame, which briefly earned me Mom of the Year with my super-fan son once he saw the photo. Would I go again? Absolutely—maybe with my own bathroom.

OUTDOOR EFFECT

THE AWE RESPONSE

MOMENTS OF AWE—HORIZON LINES, THUNDERSTORMS, VAST WATER—RESET STRESS FASTER THAN RELAXATION ALONE.
THE AMYGDALA QUIETS; PERSPECTIVE EXPANDS.

DECODER

COURAGE ≠ CONTROL
LETTING GO ISN'T LOSING POWER.
IT'S TRUSTING MOTION TO CARRY YOU FARTHER
THAN MANAGEMENT EVER COULD.

Rafting with a Football Team

On the Lower New River in West Virginia, we had a Class IV+ day that started like a postcard and turned into a lab on humility.

Our guide had the vibe of someone who's rescued a dozen people with nothing but a rope and side-eye; my boys were amped; I was in my happy place (whitewater = part adrenaline, part baptism).

Also along for the experience: three rafts of an actual college football team—coaches, players, shoulders the size of folding chairs. *Friday Night Lights: Aquatic Edition.*

First real rapid: one raft flipped clean; another ignored "high-side" and pin-wheeled. Bodies everywhere, paddles cartwheeling, that collective oh-no before instincts kick in.

A coach—full-grown, used to being in charge—swept past us, raft gone. We paddled over and hauled him in by his PFD straps. He was sopping and gasping, but also grinning: "I think I'm gonna sit in the middle for a while." My kids were wide-eyed, proud, and a little scandalized that we apparently collect adults now.

Between rapids we floated, lunched on the bank, and watched strangers become a team through smack-talk, backflips off rafts, and easy laughter. Heart rates synced with the current. The research term is *co-regulation*—how laughter and shared risk calm the nervous system faster than solitude ever could.

I didn't need data to feel it. I just knew the river was rewriting something in all of us.

Afterward, the GoPro viewing party turned chaos into community— the room full of pointing, groaning, slow-mo wipeouts, and high-fives from people who'd just been strangers in whitewater together.

Adventure didn't belong to the fittest; it belonged to the folks who showed up and shared the soak.

OUTDOOR EFFECT

FLOW + FEAR = RESILIENCE
THAT "POST-RAPIDS EUPHORIA"? IT'S CORTISOL DROPPING AND OXY-
TOCIN RISING.
FEAR METABOLIZED INTO JOY.

Lessons, Written in Mud

The outdoors isn't subtle with me. It delivers lessons with mud, chaos, and slapstick precision.

What stuck:

- Boots > bravado. Your feet will invoice you with interest. Ask me how I know: one "cute" pair of clearance boots turned a two-mile trail into a medieval blister pilgrimage.
- Sun & bugs don't negotiate. Reapply is a verb. I've returned from hikes looking like I lost a custody battle with a mosquito congregation because I forgot bug spray.
- Pack fewer "what-ifs"; pack more water and snacks. Turns out the forest does not care that I brought three kinds of backup gear but forgot the thing that keeps humans alive.
- Boats run on math. Beds ≠ bathrooms—count before you book. The time we boarded a fishing charter with one sad, communal toilet? Character building.
- Rivers reward humility. Technique + teamwork beat muscle. I once tried to brute-force my way through a current and learned that water has zero respect for ego.
- Ask for help before heroics. Launch ramps don't grade on effort. After hauling a kayak solo up a ramp in sideways rain, I now accept assistance before my spine files a complaint.

- Maps are suggestions; conditions are reality—adjust without drama. A "moderate" trail after rain is a slip-n-slide with signage. Plan accordingly.
- Laugh early. It weighs less than frustration. Every disaster gets lighter once someone snorts, "Well…this is happening."

TRAIL TRUTH

LAUGH EARLY – IT WEIGHS LESS
HUMOR DOESN'T ERASE DISCOMFORT.
IT JUST LIGHTENS THE PACK ENOUGH TO KEEP MOVING.

Each one became less a tip and more a recalibration. The longer I stayed outside, the more I noticed how my body mirrored the landscape—tight in storms, loose in sun, alert at dusk.

Scientists call that *biophilia*—our instinctive connection to living systems. I called it, finally feeling human again.

Behind the jokes are deeper truths I needed at midlife: resilience is cumulative, humility is a strength, and learning happens in the field, not the brochure. And somewhere between blisters and laughter, I realized I was less reactive everywhere else—emails, meetings, even parenting. After you've survived a night of raccoon thievery and a leaky tent, most work crises lose their teeth.

More than a Punchline

These weren't just stories to roll out at parties. They were the start of a sturdier confidence. Not the polished expert kind, but the kind you earn by trying, failing, and discovering you can survive anyway.

If you're waiting to feel ready, you'll never start. The lessons you need are hiding inside the misadventures you keep postponing.

If you are Gen X, you were raised on competence and resilience—figure it out, don't cry, don't quit. But the outdoors rewrote that script. It rewarded curiosity over control and reminded me that showing up unprepared is still showing up.

REFLECT & RESET

FIELD NOTES FROM YOUR LAST MESS
WHAT DID THE CHAOS TEACH YOU THAT NO MANUAL COULD? WRITE THE HEADLINE VERSION. KEEP IT HANDY.

FIELD NOTES

TRAIL HEROES & TOTAL ZEROES
COMPANION ESSAY AT ROOKIEOUTDOORWOMAN.COM/TRAILANDERROR.
A SALUTE TO THE REAL MVPS OF MIDLIFE MAYHEM—AND THE LESSONS THEY LEFT IN THEIR WAKE.

What Happens When You Go Off-Trail

One day, I realized *Rookie Outdoor Woman* wasn't just a name anymore. It was a voice, a way of showing up.

It hit me in the most ordinary place: my front hall. Muddy boots by the door, a damp map folded on top of my pack, two trekking poles leaning like tired sentries. On the kitchen table sat a half-written Substack draft with the working title still at the top—*What Happens Between the Cast and the Catch*—as if it belonged there.

I looked at the mess, felt the good ache in my legs, and thought: I'm not on the sidelines anymore. I'm in the game. Still clumsy. Still making mistakes that would make an REI employee sigh. But in it.

The house smelled like earth and coffee. Somewhere down the hall, the washer hummed a domestic counterpoint to the bird-song outside. For the first time in years, both sounds felt like background—not demands. I was part of the rhythm again, not the noise.

TRAIL TRUTH

YOU EARN BALANCE MID-STUMBLE
YOU DON'T WAIT FOR FOOTING.
YOU FIND IT WHILE FALLING FORWARD.

Trash Sleep, Magic Days

Camping can wreck your back and restore your brain on the same weekend.

I woke up sore and stiff, thoroughly unimpressed with my sleeping arrangement. The air had that damp-canvas smell; my hair had made its own weather system. I unzipped the tent, ready to make campfire coffee, and the morning light just…reset me.

Birds doing their shift change, a thin ribbon of mist over the water, the kind of quiet that makes your shoulders drop a full inch. I wasn't doom-scrolling. I wasn't optimizing. I was breathing like a person again.

The sleep was trash; the day was magic. That balance kept me coming back.

Later, I read that even fifteen minutes of early-morning light can recalibrate the circadian system and nudge serotonin into motion. Apparently, my body knew long before my calendar did. The tent was a chiropractor's nightmare, but the sunlight was medicine.

Trash sleep and magic days lived side by side, and once I accepted that balance, I could finally see the real pattern: the challenges and the wins weren't competing—they were shaping me. The small victories were how I learned to belong out there on my own terms, one imperfect attempt at a time.

OUTDOOR EFFECT

SUNLIGHT > SNOOZE BUTTON
NATURAL LIGHT WITHIN AN HOUR OF WAKING RESETS CIRCADIAN RHYTHMS AND LOWERS CORTISOL LEVELS.
FREE SEROTONIN DAILY.

The Wins Hidden in Plain Sight

Midlife wins don't always look like summit selfies. Sometimes they look like:

Remembering bug spray all weekend.
Friday, I made a list; Saturday, I actually used it; Sunday, I didn't look like a connect-the-dots puzzle. No one clapped. My ankles did.

Strapping the kayak without swearing (much).
I threaded the straps, tamed the flappy tails, and drove past 48 mph without the freeway kazoo. Progress sounds like quiet.

Teaching my kids the tent.
They complained. I ignored. We practiced rainfly first, guy lines second, and snack break third. The tent stood. They'll tell you they hated it. They'll also build it in eight minutes flat next time.

Tiny, ordinary wins, stacked like cairns, showed me where I'd been and that I was still moving. The same thing was happening off-trail: a hard conversation handled, a bill paid without spiraling, an evening I let myself rest.

Those micro-victories, scientists would say, train the reward system. Each tiny success flickers dopamine, teaching your brain that effort pays off. To me, it just felt like breathing space.

REFLECT & RESET

CELEBRATE THE UNIMPRESSIVE
WHAT SMALL, UN-INSTAGRAMMABLE WIN DESERVES A QUIET CHEER TODAY?
WRITE IT DOWN BEFORE YOU FORGET IT.

Belonging on My Own Terms

Those tiny wins didn't just mark progress; they stitched together a quiet sense of belonging. The more I noticed what I could do, the easier it became to see myself as someone who got to be out there in the first place.

By now, I'd learned "outdoorsy" doesn't mean perfect. It isn't elite gear, PRs, or curated grid squares. It's showing up as you are and claiming space anyway.

That shift mattered because midlife women are often gate-kept out of both fitness and outdoor spaces. Ads show twenty-somethings leaping across granite in sports bras that never ride up; trail signage and forums can read like insiders talking to insiders.

I wasn't the ad. I was a forty-nine-year-old with teenagers, a to-do list, and a good sense of humor. Belonging, it turned out, could be DIY.

The first time another hiker nodded and said, "Nice day for it," I almost looked behind me to see who she meant. Recognition, even casual, felt radical. That small exchange said what no gear label ever could: you're part of this, too.

DECODER

CONFIDENCE ≠ BELONGING
CONFIDENCE IS LOUD.
BELONGING IS STEADY—AND IT DOESN'T
NEED AN AUDIENCE.

The Beginner I Choose to Be

I still trip over roots. I still overpack snacks like we're provisioning a small expedition. I still Google *how to start a campfire without lighter fluid* and then text a friend for backup because the internet is chaos.

Classic rookie moment: I wore the wrong trail shoes to a muddy loop because they "looked more hiking-ish." Two slips later, I looked like a woodland creature who'd lost a bet.

But I laughed, learned, and saved the vanity pair for dry days. Being a rookie stopped feeling like a liability; it became my method. Curiosity over credentials. Practice over performance. Fear and excitement use the same wiring anyway. Re-label one, and suddenly the other feels possible. That's neuroscience, not pep talk.

Rookie Outdoor Woman started as a name I wasn't sure I deserved. Now it's an identity I carry proudly–not because I mastered anything, but because I didn't quit. The moment that changed things wasn't dramatic. It was me typing Rookie Outdoor Woman at the top of a draft and not backspacing. It was recognizing myself in my own mess: boots drying, coffee cooling, a story forming.

Midlife identity doesn't arrive like a lightning strike. It composts. The old stories break down and feed the new growth. The trail taught me that. Every fallen leaf becomes soil for next spring.

So yeah, I'm still a beginner. Still stumbling, still googling, still learning the hard way. But I'm here. I'm moving. And this time, I'm doing it on purpose.

OUTDOOR EFFECT

Fear ≈ Curiosity
Both light up the same brain circuits.
Reframe the adrenaline, and your body follows your story.

FIELD NOTES

"What Happens Between the Cast and the Catch"
Parallel essay on patience, practice, and the long arc of becoming—at RookieOutdoorWoman.com/trailanderror.
Because sometimes off-trail is where the story actually starts.

Part 3 Conclusion: Muddy but Moving

By the time I reached this point, I had stopped asking if I was doing it "right."

The name that once sat there unused was finally alive. My yeses, stacked one on top of the other, had carried me farther than I realized—into kayaks I couldn't lift without cursing, tents that deflated by midnight, rafts full of football players, and cabins where I discovered just how much solo space could stretch me.

It was muddy. It was chaotic. It was rarely Instagram-worthy. And it was mine.

Somewhere between the blisters and the laughter, between the river rescues and the raccoon-nightmares outside my tent, I realized I wasn't trying to become "outdoorsy" anymore. I was outdoorsy—rookie, messy, midlife, and real.

I hadn't mastered the trail, but I had mastered showing up.

That's the thing about momentum: it doesn't require grace. It just requires movement. And movement, even when it's clumsy, builds a kind of confidence that sticks.

By now, Rookie Outdoor Woman wasn't just a name I'd clicked into a blank Substack page. It was a way of being. A declaration that I was still in the game, still willing, still moving.

And the truth is, I didn't want it to end at "progress." What I wanted—what I needed—was to know I could keep going. Not just for a season, not just for a chapter. But for the long haul.

That's where the story turns next.

PART 4
STILL OUT HERE

When I realized I was in this for the long haul, I had already lost count of the missteps. Boots that blistered, tents that leaked, boats that spun in circles—I'd collected enough rookie moments to fill an entire blooper reel.

But somewhere along the way, the question shifted. It was no longer Can I do this? It became Who am I, now that I am?

The outdoors stopped being a place to prove myself and became a place to be myself. To belong, without permission slips or gate-keeping. To hike alone without apology. To claim space with snacks, awkwardness, and the stubborn kind of strength that midlife women know by heart.

This part of the story isn't about neat endings or tidy lessons. It's about pacing for seasons instead of sprints, passing on what I've learned, and remembering that the point isn't to master the trail. The point is to keep showing up—muddy, rookie, still out here.

The Long Haul

Somewhere along the way, I stopped measuring progress in days or months and started thinking in seasons.

Early on, divorce recovery came in 90-minute windows: make dinner, sign the form, don't cry in the pickup line. Later, the outdoors nudged me into a slower rhythm. I started noticing leaf edges curling to amber, the ritual of hauling bins from the hall closet and tucking them back again, washing fall hoodies like punctuation marks on a week.

I didn't plan that shift; it arrived the way dusk does–gradually, then all at once. The seasons gave me a language for patience that therapy handouts never could.

DECODER

PATIENCE ≠ PAUSE
WAITING ISN'T DOING NOTHING.
IT'S LETTING TIME DO ITS HALF OF THE WORK.

Fishing as Reset

We fished with rocks, holding our rods in place. One TV channel. An outhouse. Like a lot of Gen X, I didn't grow up *outdoorsy*–I grew up *outside*. The magic wasn't the fish; it was the waiting, the laughing, the being together.

That memory found me again as an adult on the dock of a small lake, cheap rod across my knees, a tub of nightcrawlers sweating in the shade. We baited hooks, cast sloppily, and settled into the old timing: watch the line, tell a story, forget the story halfway through, pick it up again. A heron lifted slowly from the far bank. The boys argued about whether the bobber twitched (it didn't).

We didn't pull anything brag-worthy from the water, but my pulse stopped sprinting. Fishing, it turns out, is a metaphor for midlife patience and parenting teenagers: set the line, give some slack, try not to thrash when nothing moves for a while.

On the days when home felt like triage, we'd walk around the neighborhood lake and let the quiet do the heavy lifting. There's a specific kind of mercy in watching ripples make their slow V across the surface as the light goes the color of honey. The gnats try to ruin it and fail.

I didn't know the biology then, only that water kept quietly maintaining my nervous system. Later, I learned there's a name for that steadying: Blue Mind. Being near water lowers cortisol within minutes, nudges the vagus nerve into calm mode, and gives the brain a kind of soft-focus clarity. Which explains why even a tiny trout, a broken pole, and the loss of a beloved pair of sunglasses still sent me home smiling. The reset never came from the catch. It came from the current.

Eventually, I started gaming the system. A desktop loop of river noise while I graded. A cheap tabletop fountain on my desk. A longer shower on the days the to-do list tried to audition as a villain. None of it is fancy, but all of it is effective.

Whether it's a lake, a creek, a shower, or a badly tied bobber, water says the same thing: breathe, wait, soften a little. The current will keep moving. You can, too.

OUTDOOR EFFECT

THE CAST-AND-CALM LOOP

REPETITIVE MOTIONS—CASTING, PADDLING, WALKING—NUDGE THE BRAIN INTO ALPHA-WAVE CALM.

YOUR NERVOUS SYSTEM LOVES A RHYTHM MORE THAN A RESULT.

FIELD NOTES

BLUE MIND STARTER GUIDE

EXPLORE THE RESEARCH BEHIND WATER-BASED CALM AT ROOKIEOUTDOORWOMAN.COM/TRAILANDERROR.

SIMPLE WAYS TO BRING THE RIPPLE EFFECT HOME.

Trees as Medicine

For my fiftieth birthday, I gave myself a week off and a tiny cabin with no electronics. I wandered quiet trails, made small fires, and sat long enough for the static to thin. Somewhere between pine needles and smoke, a different milestone landed: I finished a full draft of this book. Not with balloons, but with dirt on my boots and words that finally behaved. Forest bathing, it turns out, is creativity's best unpaid intern.

It isn't woo—trees exhale phytoncides, our nervous systems exhale back. Blood pressure drops. Breath evens. Attention returns. You don't need miles; you need presence. A park bench counts.

There was a downed trunk shaped like an armchair. I sat. The bark pressed a grid into my calves. Sun freckles dappled my notebook. Somewhere, a wood thrush played the same four notes like it was reassuring the understory. Pages that had been stubborn for months finally slid into place. Not because I tried harder, but because I stopped bracing.

OUTDOOR EFFECT

STAND AMONG TREES, BREATHE
FOREST TIME LOWERS CORTISOL AND BOOSTS IMMUNE MARKERS. FIVE MINUTES IS ENOUGH TO START.

Seasons of Trying

I stopped chasing quick wins and started noticing cycles.

Fall: Leaf-crackle underfoot, air with a bite, me walking farther without bargaining. My pack is lighter, and so is my mind. I learned which creeks shrink to polite threads and which hold their voices after the first cold snap.

Winter: Shorter walks, longer soups, two mugs steaming by the window—quiet company while the creek kept talking. On bright days, the bare canopy turned trails into cathedral aisles; on gray ones, the color scale narrowed to pewter and pine, and my breath drew soft clouds like punctuation.

Summer: Heat and bugs and laughter. Kayak straps that finally behaved. Evening hikes that ended sticky, tired, but happy. I stopped chasing noon and aimed for edges—dawn's mercy, dusk's longer shadows—accepting that the season asks for slowness and electrolytes, not heroics.

Spring: Mud and optimism. Plans scribbled on a calendar, half of them crossed out, all of them pointing toward "keep going." I forgot trails could smell like rain and leaf buds, like an apology for February. The first frog chorus each year felt like a standing ovation for simply showing up.

The seasons outside mapped onto the seasons inside: bursts of energy, lulls, messy middles. None of it is wrong, but all is part of the arc.

I began to realize how much biology had to say about this: every major organ follows a circadian rhythm; recovery does too. Rest isn't laziness, it's synchronization.

REFLECT & RESET

Check Your Season

Which season are you in right now—growth, stillness, rebuild, rest?

What does it need from you, instead of what do you owe it?

The Long View

This wasn't about becoming an expert or collecting merit badges. It was about staying in it.

The long haul asks less for speed than for stubbornness—the kind that shows up in damp weather and tries again when plans shift.

Sometimes, stubborn looks like lacing up even when the sky threatens rain. Sometimes it's admitting you'd rather read the map from the car but unfolding it anyway.

Midlife women don't need faster fixes; we need durable practices. Walking counts. Sitting by water counts. Laughing at a miscast counts. The rebuild doesn't happen in a weekend; it happens in repetitions.

On a trip that tried to go sideways—forgotten bug spray, wrong turn, thunder muttering—I set a 15-minute rule: if it's still miserable in fifteen, I bail. It wasn't. The storm shouldered past; the trail opened to a small overlook I'd have sworn wasn't on the map. Sometimes grit is just agreeing to renegotiate with the weather.

TRAIL TRUTH

DURABILITY > DISCIPLINE
KEEP SHOWING UP, EVEN CROOKED.
CONSISTENCY IS ITS OWN KIND OF GRACE.

Still Going

The work wasn't to be finished quickly. The work was to keep going.

By my door: muddy boots airing out, laces looped over the rail. In the corner: rods propped like exclamation points. On the counter: a little stack—snack restock, sunscreen tossed in, a folded map spotted with coffee.

I wipe dirt from the soles, rinse a reel, and throw wet socks straight into the wash (lesson learned). None of it glamorous. All of it mine.

Each motion—rinse, fold, restock—became a mindfulness drill disguised as housekeeping. Even cleaning gear kept me tethered to the life I'd built from the ruins.

I started ending outings with a five-minute "closeout": empty the pack, lay everything out to dry, and jot down two lines in the margin of a calendar about what worked and what didn't. It sounds fussy. It isn't. It's future-me care, and she is very grateful.

And when the next season turns, I'll still be here—rookie, steady, showing up.

Because the long haul isn't a finish line; it's the comfort of still belonging to your own momentum.

FIELD NOTES

STILL OUT HERE
FINAL REFLECTIONS ON PERSISTENCE AND PEACE—HOW TO STAY ROOTED WHEN THE STORY QUIETS.
READ AT ROOKIEOUTDOORWOMAN.COM/TRAILANDERROR.

CHAPTER 16

Life After the Storm Isn't Just Sunshine

For a long time, I thought someone else had to stamp my ticket before I belonged outdoors.

In my head, *belonging* sounded like a test: fluent in gear-speak, approved by a ranger, invited by people who camped at altitude for fun. I half expected a uniformed official to ask for my credentials at a trailhead (he never did). Slowly, the shift came: no one was keeping score but me.

The trail didn't check IDs. It just asked if I would show up.

DECODER

BELONGING ≠ VALIDATION
APPROVAL IS A MOVING TARGET.
BELONGING STARTS THE MOMENT YOU STOP WAITING FOR
SOMEONE ELSE TO HAND YOU A PASS.

Outdoor Gatekeeping

On my phone: perfect grid squares—glossy tents, latte foam in enamel mugs, and women with hair that doesn't frizz under headlamps.

In my car: a chaotic trunk—muddy boots, a crumpled map, three kinds of snacks, and the confidence of a woman who knows bug spray is more important than matching anything.

I had absorbed the message that "outdoorsy" was a club: own the right pack, wear the right layers, quote the right topo lines…then you may proceed.

Reality: if you step outside with intention, curiosity, and maybe some snacks, you're outdoorsy.

I remember scrolling through reels of mountain vistas, watching 20-somethings leap over streams in slow motion, and wondering if the algorithm had ever met humidity or hot flashes. The feeds looked polished; I looked like a damp field note. It took me a while to realize that there's more authenticity in mud-streaked shins than in filtered summits.

A three-day backpacking trip counts. So does a lap of your neighborhood park in Crocs. Perfection never stamped belonging; participation did.

TRAIL TRUTH

PRESENCE > PERMISSION
YOU DON'T NEED CREDENTIALS TO BELONG OUTSIDE.
JUST CURIOSITY AND A SNACK.

Finding Freedom in Solitude

After spending years dodging outdoor gatekeeping and everyone else's opinions about how I *should* hike, camp, or exist, I realized something simple: the minute you stop performing for other people, the trail opens up in a whole new way. Breaking free from all that noise makes room for actual exploration–the kind that starts on the inside before your boots even hit the dirt.

Ever tried hiking with teenagers? Less majestic wildlife, more chorus of complaints. Solitude, it turns out, wasn't loneliness–it was freedom.

One morning on a quiet loop, I set out alone. The air was cool enough to make breath visible. My footsteps found a rhythm; birds stitched sound through the pines; a woodpecker hammered somewhere out of sight. No one asked about Wi-Fi. No one needed a snack at minute six.

The light that morning had a kindness to it–diffused through fog, soft on everything it touched. The smell of wet pine hit that part of my brain that still believes in summer camp and second chances. Somewhere between the crunch of gravel and the heartbeat in my ears, I felt something I hadn't in months: unclenched.

I paused at a small overlook–nothing dramatic, just a slice of water through trees–and felt the kind of exhale that had been hard to find in my own house. Hiking alone lets me set the pace of my body and my thoughts.

It was the opposite of isolation; it was reunion.

OUTDOOR EFFECT

THE RESTORATION REFLEX
SOFT SIGHTS–WATER, LEAVES, CLOUDS–DROP BRAINWAVE FREQUENCY AND REFILL ATTENTION.
STILLNESS IS MEDICINE DISGUISED AS SCENERY.

Scientists call this *attention restoration*–the mind resets when we switch from screens to soft fascination, like ripples or wind through branches. I didn't need the terminology then. I just knew I could finally hear myself think.

Walking Alone, Not Unprepared

Solo doesn't mean alone. It means self-reliant. And that's powerful.

I started carrying what made me steady: water, a whistle, a small light, a bandana, a charger, and the map actually downloaded (rookie-to-pro move).

On a humid afternoon, a spur trail I swore would reconnect... didn't. For a beat, my chest did that fluttery panic thing. Then the basics: stop, breathe, check blazes, check the map, backtrack to the last certainty. Ten calm minutes later, the main trail appeared as if it had been there all along.

Preparedness wasn't paranoia. It was trust I could borrow from myself when my brain got loud.

Later, I learned why breathing helped. Deep inhales activate the vagus nerve–the body's built-in brake pedal. Even one slow exhale can drop your heart rate and trick your nervous system into believing you're safe, which is sometimes half the battle.

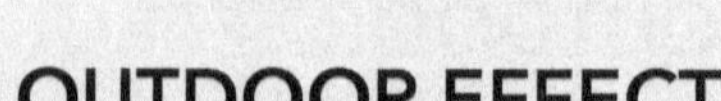

OUTDOOR EFFECT

PRACTICE CALM UNDER TREES
TRAINING YOUR STRESS RESPONSE OUTSIDE REWIRES THE BRAIN TO LINK EFFORT WITH SAFETY.
CHALLENGE + SERENITY = RESILIENCE.

Merit Badge, Midlife Edition

Halfway through a trail in Uwharrie, the forest went still in that way it sometimes does—like someone hit the mute button on the world. No birds, no breeze, just me and the crunch of my boots on leaf litter. That's when I saw it: a berry-studded pile in the middle of the path. Too big for a rabbit. Too plant-heavy for a deer.

My brain did a quick nature math problem: size, contents, location. Then came the internal monologue only a woman hiking solo can produce—equal parts curiosity, caution, and self-coaching. *Okay. Probably bear. Probably old. Probably fine. Please don't let this be the prologue to a Dateline episode.*

I crouched, snapped a photo like a responsible citizen scientist-slash-weirdo, and did what any modern naturalist does: Googled. The search history now reads, *What does bear poop look like,* which is how I learned it's technically called scat, and that mine (the pile's, not mine) was textbook black bear.

I did not sprint for civilization. I did not pull a muscle looking over my shoulder. I kept walking—heart rate slightly elevated, but posture intact. Confidence, it turns out, sometimes starts with a well-timed field note and a decision not to spiral.

What surprised me wasn't the discovery; it was the calm that followed. My body did the sensible scan for movement and sound, then relaxed. I wasn't helpless out there—I was observant. And that shift, from fear to awareness, was worth more than any souvenir.

Somewhere between curiosity and composure, I earned my most unlikely badge yet.

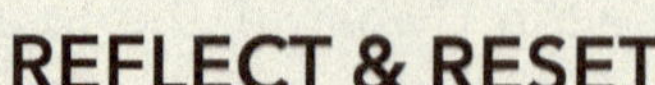

REFLECT & RESET

THE CALM YOU EARNED
REMEMBER THE LAST TIME YOU CAUGHT YOURSELF STEADY INSTEAD OF SPIRALING.
WRITE DOWN WHAT YOU DID RIGHT—SO NEXT TIME YOU'LL TRUST IT FASTER.

Midlife Belonging

Outdoor marketing rarely shows women at midlife. No perimenopause jokes in gear catalogs. No backpacking models with laugh lines or teenagers off-camera asking where the towels went. In most campaigns, we're either invisible or reduced to "supportive mom who packed the snacks." Culture likes us in helper roles: caretakers, planners, reliable background characters who make other people's adventures possible.

And the erasure isn't just something we imagine. REI's *Outside In* report found that 63 percent of women believe outdoor media "rarely or never" shows people who look like them (REI, 2017). A later Merrell/Seek More survey echoed this, with over half of women saying they feel underrepresented or misrepresented, and 68 percent stating that lack of representation makes new activities feel less accessible (Merrell, *Outside Voices*, 2022). For midlife women, the gap widens: AARP's 2023 media report found that only 6 percent of images featuring women outdoors included anyone over forty.

The Gen X conditioning doesn't help. Be competent. Be useful. Be low maintenance. We were the latchkey generation; independence was survival, not self-care. We learned to handle things quietly, carry emotional backpacks heavier than anything at REI, and not inconvenience anyone with our needs. So the first time

I stepped into the woods with no agenda, no audience, and no role to perform, it felt almost subversive.

There, I wasn't anyone's employee, parent, or partner. I was just a mammal with good boots and questionable snacks.

Claiming the outdoors in midlife felt both radical and ordinary. Radical because I put myself in the frame. Ordinary because I was just…there. Walking. Sweating. Laughing. Coming back next weekend.

And representation matters in measurable ways. According to the Outdoor Industry Association, women who see relatable role models in outdoor media report a 33 percent increase in confidence and a 25 percent increase in likelihood to try a new activity (OIA, 2021).

Turns out visibility isn't cosmetic—it's psychological infrastructure. It changes behavior. Belonging changes access.

There's quiet defiance in midlife women taking up space in places that don't always expect us, on trails, in boardrooms, or even during rest. Belonging isn't a prize handed out at the finish line; it's the ground you stand on when you stop apologizing for being there.

REFLECT & RESET

SHOW UP BEFORE YOU FEEL READY
THINK OF ONE PLACE YOU'VE DELAYED GOING UNTIL YOU "QUALIFIED."
GO ANYWAY.
BELONGING STARTS WITH ARRIVAL, NOT APPROVAL.

I stopped waiting for permission slips. I stopped waiting for someone to call me outdoorsy. I belonged because I was there.

FIELD NOTES

MIDLIFE BELONGING GUIDE
RESOURCES AND REFLECTIONS FOR WOMEN CLAIMING SPACE OUTDOORS AND EVERYWHERE ELSE.
FIND IT AT ROOKIEOUTDOORWOMAN.COM/TRAILANDERROR.

CHAPTER 17

Passing It On

The outdoors handed me back pieces of myself I didn't know I'd misplaced. Eventually, it hit me: this was never meant to stay mine. What I was learning out there was something I'd carry forward and offer others.

That realization hit during a quiet moment after I published a *Rookie Outdoor Woman* post. I closed the laptop, poured coffee, and looked at my muddy boots by the door–the same ones that had carried me through wobble and doubt–and thought: okay, this is how legacy starts. Not with a speech. With one person trying because you said it was okay to be new.

The messages kept pinging–small, digital echoes of courage. It wasn't vanity; it was recognition. Proof that stories travel farther than shoes ever could.

DECODER

LEGACY ≠ MONUMENT
YOU DON'T HAVE TO BUILD SOMETHING GRAND.
IT'S ENOUGH TO LEAVE FOOTPRINTS SOMEONE
ELSE CAN FIND.

West Virginia: The SOS That Wasn't

On a ridge above the New River, one son and I got–let's call it– re-oriented. The plan was a tidy loop. The reality was a bonus tour.

We came out at a road that climbed straight up like it had a grudge. My calves issued a formal complaint; my teenager declared, accurately, that this road was rude.

So we phoned the other son–both boys had learner permits then–and asked for a slow-roll rescue. He crept the car down the mountain like he was chauffeuring a sleeping beehive, hands at ten and two, the picture of DMV-approved composure.

"Don't tell anyone you called your kid to pick you up," he said, deadpan.

"Oh, I'm absolutely telling everyone," I said. "It's called using your resources."

The windows were down; the air smelled like pine and relief. Somewhere below, the river shimmered, proof that we hadn't been lost, just redirected.

Legacy, it turns out, can look like asking for help–and letting your kid be the hero.

TRAIL TRUTH

LEGACY STARTS WITH ONE YES
YOU DON'T HAVE TO BLAZE A TRAIL–JUST POINT
SOMEONE TOWARD THEIRS.

The Mines (a.k.a. Are We There Yet, Appalachia Edition)

Another day, I lured them toward abandoned mines because–history! Mystery! Photo ops!

Ten minutes in: "How much longer?"
Fifteen: "Is this the last hill?"
Twenty: "Does this path even go anywhere?"

The chorus of complaints was relentless and extremely on brand.

We did make it—rusted timbers, cool air sliding from the dark mouth of the shaft, a hush that made us instinctively lower our voices. For a sliver of a minute, they were quiet, taking it in. Then:

"Okay, that was cool. Can we get pizza?"

Not cinematic. Perfect anyway.

As we descended, the light filtered through the gold-green canopy, the smell of rain on iron. They weren't scrolling; they were present. That's all any parent really wants—a shared beat of awareness before the world rushes back in.

Those flashes taught me something I wish I'd learned sooner: passing it on doesn't always look like enthusiasm. Sometimes it's exposure. Seeds don't sprout on schedule; they sprout when they're ready.

And that lesson carried straight into the next adventure—different place, same truth about what we remember and why.

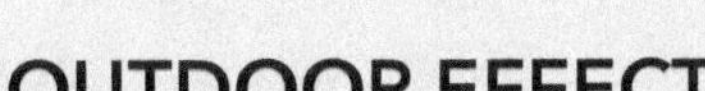

OUTDOOR EFFECT

Awe → Generosity
Moments of wonder lower stress hormones and increase empathy.
Even brief awe makes people kinder.

Ghosts and Reveille

Adventure doesn't always mean pine needles. Sometimes it smells like diesel fuel and starts at 0600.

We signed up for an overnight on a decommissioned aircraft carrier—a floating museum now, docked for tourists and Scout troops brave enough to sleep inside a steel echo chamber. The brochure promised "a night aboard history," which sounded charming in a brochure way. I packed earplugs and optimism.

The ship loomed gray and massive against the sunset, the air thick with salt and engine ghosts. Inside, the temperature dropped and the smell hit—metal, oil, a faint cafeteria nostalgia. Every sound reverberated. Boots clanged. Laughter ricocheted. Even whispers had acoustics.

Sleeping quarters were split by gender. I lucked into the officers' section—narrow bunks, but real mattresses. The boys got the enlisted triple stacks, three layers of claustrophobia with a ladder you could stub your soul on.

A docent appeared, and suddenly every creak became a narrative. Pipes hissed like whispered warnings. I stayed awake half the night rehearsing my apology to whatever Navy spirit still took attendance.

And then—0600.
Reveille.

It blasted from the loudspeakers with the force of a brass section auditioning for judgment day. Scouts thundered overhead. My nervous system submitted its resignation.

But once the chaos settled, the absurdity became its own kind of magic: mess-hall coffee that was both terrible and sacred, a submarine tour that tested our commitment to oxygen, and after-hours roaming through floodlit decks while the river lapped below. The boys made up call signs; I tried not to think about the ghost. We laughed our way through the night and retold every moment over powdered eggs at dawn.

Different settings—Appalachian mines, an echoing steel giant—same lesson: adventure rarely looks like the brochure. What stays with us isn't perfection; it's presence. It's the moments when our kids forget to perform adulthood-in-progress and just *exist* beside us. Passing it on isn't about orchestrating awe. It's about creating conditions where awe can surprise us all.

REFLECT & RESET

SHARED CHAOS COUNTS
THINK OF ONE ADVENTURE—MESSY, FUNNY, OR FAILED—THAT TURNED INTO A STORY EVERYONE STILL TELLS.
THAT'S BELONGING IN MOTION.

Teaching by Doing

My boys were outdoorsy before I was. Scouts since they could tie their own shoes, they'd camped through thunderstorms, earned badges for everything from fire-building to first aid, and could identify poison ivy at a hundred yards while I was still Googling "three leaves shiny?"

They had patches. I had questions.

So when I started hiking again, they were patient in that teenage, good-natured way—equal parts pride and amusement. "Need help with your tent, Mom?" one would ask, already holding the pole I'd misthreaded. Their skills came from years of Scout weekends; mine came from stubbornness and trial by YouTube.

I stopped preaching about resilience and started modeling it.

They saw me misread a junction, breathe, and backtrack. They saw me wrestle a stuck strap, step aside, try again, and ask a stranger for help. Old me would've hidden the mistakes. New me narrates the recovery:

"Okay, that's on me. Next step–find a blaze, confirm the map, try again."

That was the lesson: not to *be perfect,* but to *keep going.*

And it turns out, Scouts are fluent in that language. They already knew the motto–*be prepared.* I was learning the sequel–*stay present.*

They saw me rebuild alone and, later, choose a partner who adds steadiness but doesn't replace it. That's also part of the inheritance: showing them what partnership looks like when it's built on mutual capability, not rescue.

A Midlife Inheritance

We talk about leaving money, heirlooms, and diplomas.

I want to leave something else:

- Permission to take up space.
- A model of resilience that includes course corrections.
- The memory of their mom muddy, sweaty, laughing–and still trying.

Call it a midlife inheritance: cycle-breaking in hiking boots.

Especially for sons, it matters to see women claim joy, strength, and adventure beyond service roles. It recalibrates what normal looks like. When they see their mom lacing up, packing her own gear, and walking back into the woods she once feared, it rewires more than expectations–it rewires empathy.

When we teach resilience through embodiment, not lectures, our kids absorb nervous system safety–the felt sense that it's okay to fail and still be loved. That's neuroscience, not sentiment.

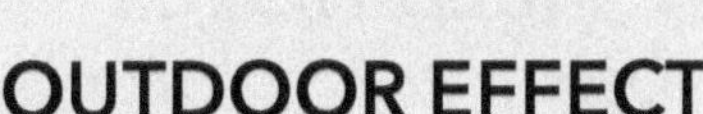

OUTDOOR EFFECT

THE BIOLOGY OF BELONGING
CO-REGULATED CALM—SEEING SOMEONE RECOVER INSTEAD OF IMPLODE—TEACHES SAFETY FASTER THAN WORDS.

Forward Into Legacy

Passing it on never meant handing over a perfect map. It meant showing that maps are helpful, not holy.

On the last evening of our West Virginia trip, the boys walked ahead, shoulders almost brushing, tossing jokes I couldn't quite hear. The trail was a corridor of golden light, the air thick with pine and the faint sweetness of a distant campfire. My pack was lighter than usual; I'd given them most of the snacks.

I watched them move down the trail–confident, unhurried–and realized legacy isn't what you leave behind; it's what walks ahead of you, carrying granola bars and a sense of belonging. Watching them find their own footing reminded me that the best things we pass on are those shaped by shared experience–laughter, struggle, and the courage to step into the unknown anyway.

The outdoors gave me a story. They gave it continuity.

And that's the inheritance I care about most: not the patches they earned or the trails I conquered, but the way those two stories now overlap.

Legacy means making sure they—and the women reading along—
know they can write theirs, too.

FIELD NOTES

PASSING IT ON
PRACTICAL WAYS TO SHARE THE TRAIL—MENTORING, MICRO-ADVEN-
TURES, AND MODELING COURAGE.
FIND IT AT ROOKIEOUTDOORWOMAN.COM/TRAILANDERROR.

CHAPTER 18

Still Out Here

There isn't a finish line for this.
It doesn't get wrapped up in a neat bow (or Scout knot).
It's one more trail, one more yes, one more story.

I didn't set out to become an "outdoors woman."
I set out to survive. To breathe.
To find space when my life felt like it was collapsing.

What I didn't expect was how survival would stretch into something steadier—growth layered over grit, endurance built one imperfect mile at a time.

And yet, here I am.

Still out here.

TRAIL TRUTH

THE FINISH LINE IS FICTION
HEALING DOESN'T ANNOUNCE ITSELF WITH MEDALS.
IT SHOWS UP IN MOTION—BOOTS ON DIRT, BREATH STEADY,
STORY STILL UNFOLDING.

Then / Now / The Long Game

The long game of hiking became the long game of becoming—patience, grit, and the willingness to keep showing up.

Then: a picnic table in a city park, me staring at trees to borrow their breathing. I remember gripping the edge of the table, watching a dog track a squirrel, the air thick with cut grass and grill smoke. The branches swayed like they were exhaling for me when I couldn't.

Then: a solo beach week with only the tide and coffee on the agenda. I woke to gulls screeching and the steady pulse of waves, my mug warm against my palms as I watched the water flatten and unflatten itself. The days stretched long and quiet, the kind that soften you without asking permission.

Then: a first hike that ended in blisters and a muttered "never again." I limped the last half-mile, sweat mixing with equal parts frustration and stubborn pride. My heels burned, my pack dug into my shoulders, and every root felt like a personal attack. I sat in the car afterward with my shoes off, equal parts wrecked and weirdly proud.

Then I walked as if I were being chased. Now I walk like I'm arriving.

Same woman, different nervous system—boots that fit, water packed, map downloaded, a quiet confidence humming beneath the rookie nerves.

I still take breaks on benches. I still cry at shorelines. But I don't doubt I belong on the path to get there.

Somewhere along the way, the outdoors stopped being an escape and became endurance—a long conversation between my body and the world around it.

The miles became prayers I didn't have to word.

I caught myself one day walking without the old commentary–no checklist, no performance review–just the punctuation of steps and breath. That's neuroplasticity in hiking boots: repetition teaches the body safety until the mind finally believes it. If you're curious about the science behind that, discover more on neuro-plasticity and why repeated movement rewires the brain at the link in the footnote below.[2]

The work was never about summits or pace. It was about staying in it.

Because healing isn't a sprint–it's a sediment process, layer by layer, moment by moment.

Seasons change. Life shifts. The outdoors stay.

Too many midlife women vanish from adventure stories–or get written out altogether.

My rookie journey became a kind of reclamation project: a way of proving that middle age isn't the epilogue. It's the rewrite.

OUTDOOR EFFECT

MOVEMENT REWIRES CALM

REPETITIVE MOTION IN GREEN SPACES LOWERS CORTISOL AND BOOSTS SEROTONIN–THE NERVOUS SYSTEM'S WAY OF WRITING CALM INTO MUSCLE MEMORY.

I'll always be a rookie.

---

2 Tworek, Grace. "What Is Neuroplasticity? How It Works." Cleveland Clinic, December 12, 2023. https://health.clevelandclinic.org/neuroplasticity.

Nature keeps humbling me: new gear to misassemble, new trails to underestimate, new rivers to nudge me sideways.

Recent rookie: left bug spray on the counter–became an all-you-can-eat special.
Future rookie (seventy-year-old me): mismatched poles, pockets full of gummy bears, telling anyone who'll listen that *reapply* is a verb.

Every mistake still startles a laugh out of me, and laughter is proof I'm not performing–I'm participating. Humility is good for your vagus nerve.

Each mile strengthens belonging until it feels less like a prize and more like a muscle.
And that's the long game: persistence as peace.

REFLECT & RESET

THE LONG GAME
LIST ONE SMALL RHYTHM THAT KEEPS YOU STEADY–WALKING, JOURNALING, MORNING COFFEE.
CALL IT TRAINING FOR PEACE. DO IT AGAIN TOMORROW.

The Outdoors as Religion

I don't believe in church the way I did when I was young.

But the forest? The water? That's where I find my rituals.

My communion table is a weathered log. My hymns are birds fluting in the canopy and the long sigh of wind through pines.

After my dad died, I hiked the waterfalls he loved. Mist settled on my face like a blessing. Grief didn't leave; it sat down beside me and stopped insisting I carry it alone.

That's what this sanctuary does—it holds what I can't.

I don't pray for outcomes anymore. I listen for alignment. The forest answers in echoes; the river answers in momentum. Faith, I've realized, doesn't always sound like hope—it often sounds like the steady rhythm of feet on a trail you finally trust.

Sometimes I look at my sons, now grown and taller than me, and think of all the places that carried us—how the woods became our cathedral, the water our shared baptism, the trail our family pew.

They learned reverence without anyone naming it. We all did.

OUTDOOR EFFECT

AWE AS ANCHOR
REPEATED AWE MOMENTS—LIGHT THROUGH TREES, WAVES AT DUSK—
CALM THE AMYGDALA AND STRENGTHEN GRATITUDE CIRCUITS.
WONDER IS A RENEWABLE RESOURCE.

An Invitation

Rookie Outdoor Woman was never just my story.
It's a hand outstretched.

If you've ever felt too late, too clumsy, too uncertain—you belong out here too.

Bring snacks, not perfection.
Bring curiosity, not credentials.

Start with a bench, a loop, a shoreline.

Say yes once. Then again.

And if you wander away for a while–life, work, weather, whatever–know this:
The outdoors keeps no ledger. It won't scold or shame you for the absence. It just says, "Hey, you came back."

That kind of forgiveness is rare. That's why I keep returning.

This community of midlife women who lace up anyway–who learn the constellations of their courage through scraped knees and stubborn optimism–reminds me daily that resilience isn't solitary. I've watched women guide each other through first hikes, divorces, job changes, and grief. Shared miles became shared metaphors. It turns out we weren't just finding trails–we were finding each other.

It's shared.

Every time one of us says, "I tried," another whispers, "Me too." That's how the circle widens.

REFLECT & RESET

THE INVITATION YOU NEEDED
WHO COULD USE PERMISSION RIGHT NOW—THE SAME WAY YOU ONCE DID?
SEND THEM A MESSAGE, OR JUST LEAD BY EXAMPLE.
THAT'S HOW THE TRAIL KEEPS GROWING.

So if you ever need proof that you belong out here, picture this: a slightly mud-splattered woman waving from the bend in the trail, snacks in her pack, ready to walk beside you for a mile or two.

Trail Marker

I started by craving space. I end by claiming it.

By my door: muddy boots drying, a map with coffee freckles, and a Ziploc of gummy bears refilled on purpose.

Out there: waves keeping time, blazes winking from the next turn, a path that isn't asking for proof—only presence.

At first, the outdoors was survival. Then movement. Then momentum. Finally, rhythm.

The trail taught me what life had been whispering all along: you don't need a map to move forward. You just need to start—to stumble, to laugh, to get muddy, and to try again.

Still forgetting tie-downs sometimes. Still startling raccoons on night watch. Still pushing boats off logs—and laughing when I slip.

Still a rookie.
Still learning.
Still out here.

And maybe that's the whole point.

FIELD NOTES

STILL OUT HERE
BONUS REFLECTIONS AND READER STORIES FROM THE *ROOKIE OUTDOOR WOMAN* COMMUNITY.
FIND THEM AT ROOKIEOUTDOORWOMAN.COM/TRAILANDERROR.

rookieoutdoorwoman.com/**trailanderror**

About the Author

Heidi S. Bonner, PhD, is a professor, researcher, and late-blooming adventurer who believes it's never too late to start over–or start outside. As Department Chair and Professor of Criminal Justice and Criminology at East Carolina University, she has spent more than twenty years studying leadership, decision-making, and systems of accountability designed to protect others. Her work has been supported by the National Institute of Justice, the Office on Violence Against Women, and the Robert Wood Johnson Foundation, among others, and has shaped national conversations on public safety, wellness, and organizational leadership.

Beyond academia, Heidi is the founder of Rookie Outdoor Woman, a writing and lifestyle platform dedicated to helping Gen X, Boomer, and older Millennial women reconnect with confidence and curiosity through the outdoors. Her essays and guides blend humor, honesty, and practical advice, reminding readers that adventure has no age limit and "perfect" is never the goal. Through her Substack and website, she's built a growing community of women who are done waiting for the right time and ready to trade "too late" for "let's go."

Before founding Rookie Outdoor Woman, Heidi spent over a decade leading teams, mentoring students, and consulting for public-safety organizations. She is also the founder of Word Sleuth Copywriting, LLC, where she helps mission-driven companies and public-safety vendors translate their complex work into clear, human-centered stories that connect with the people they serve.

Her book, *Trail and Error: A Rookie Outdoor Woman's Guide to Reclaiming Life and Confidence After 50*, is part memoir, part manifesto, and all heart. Drawing on her experiences as a researcher, leader, and self-proclaimed "rookie," Heidi explores what it means to rebuild identity, rediscover joy, and embrace imperfection—one trail (and error) at a time.

When she's not teaching, writing, or testing her gear for Rookie Outdoor Woman, you can find Heidi kayaking, hiking, or planning her next not-entirely-graceful outdoor experiment. Heidi lives in North Carolina, co-parenting her twin sons and proving that curiosity and courage are the best survival skills of all.

9 798999 382761 2